ESSENTIAL

OPPORTUNITY CLASS

THINKING SKILLS

5 Thinking Skills Test Papers

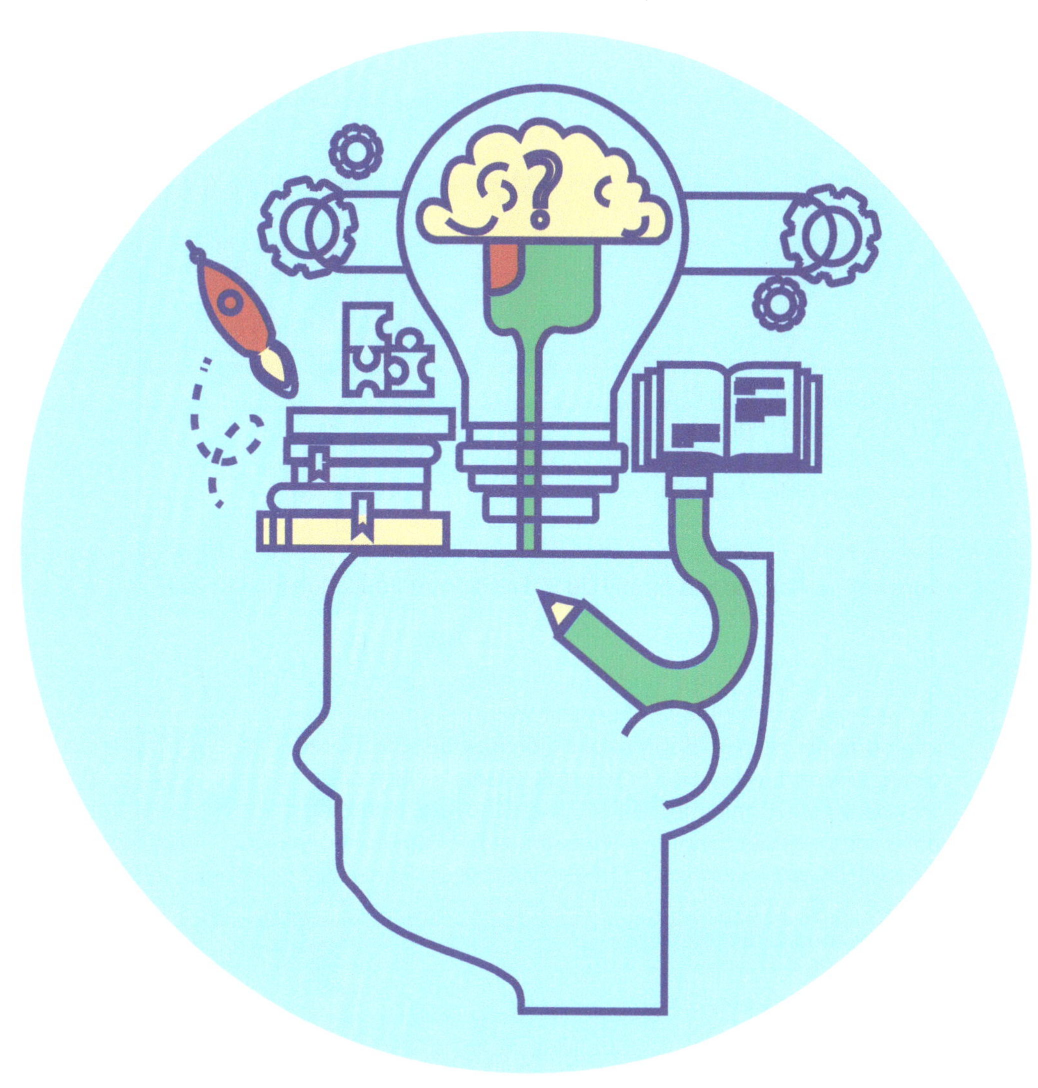

RAY LEE | JIMMY LIU

To Cookie, my light,
and to Phoebe who I hope
can one day figure out all the questions in this book.

Five Senses Education Pty Ltd
2/195 Prospect Highway
Seven Hills 2147
New South Wales Australia

First Published 2023

Lee, Ray and Liu, Jimmy

Essential Opportunity Class
Thinking Skills Book 2
ISBN 978-1-76032-539-8

2023 02 20

Contents

Preface

This book is designed to help students prepare for the Opportunity Class Placement Test. It consists of five thinking skills practice exam papers and is suitable for use by Year 3 and 4 students. The exam papers are designed to the exact format of the Opportunity Class Placement Test, with hand picked questions that closely relate to past Opportunity Class Examination questions.

Success in this extremely competitive exam requires commitment and hard work. We hope these practice exam papers can help you achieve your goals.

Five Senses Education

OC Practice Test Paper

Thinking Skills 6 (Time allowed: 30 min)

INSTRUCTIONS

1. Write your Name on the cover page.
2. There are **30** questions in this paper. For each question there are four possible answers, **A**, **B**, **C** and **D**. Choose the **one** correct answer and record your choice on the separate answer sheet. If you make a mistake, erase thoroughly and try again.
3. You will **not** lose marks for incorrect answers, so you should attempt **all 30** questions
4. You **must** complete the answer sheet within the time limit. There will **not** be any extra time at the end of the exam to record your answers on the answer sheet.
5. You can use the question paper for working out, but no extra paper is allowed.
6. Calculators and dictionaries are **NOT** allowed.

Name: ____

1 "I think you'll like your present, Scott. You'll still be able to use it for at least the next couple of months before the weather gets too warm. It can be a lot of fun, especially if you take a lesson or two first. Remember, people are often injured by using these things if they don't know what they're doing."

What conclusion can be drawn from the passage?

A Scott's new present is a Rifle

B Scott's new present is a Tennis Racquet

C Scott's new present is a Snow Shovel

D Scott's new present is a Snowboard

2 Three children like three different types of fruit; lemon, bananas, and oranges. Given that Norris dislikes oranges and bananas, Shirley hates all foods yellow, and Megan likes?

A oranges

B bananas

C lemon

D not enough information

3 The first little pig was very lazy. He didn't want to work at all so he built his house out of straw. The second little pig worked a little bit harder but he was somewhat lazy too so he built his house out of sticks. Then, they sang and danced and played together the rest of the day.

Which of the following is an assumption made by the above argument?

A The third little pig made his house out of bricks

B The 3 pigs danced

C Straw is not a good material to make houses

D Stick is the worst material to make houses out of

4 This is what the angle between the minute hand and the hour hand of the clock looks like at 3:30.

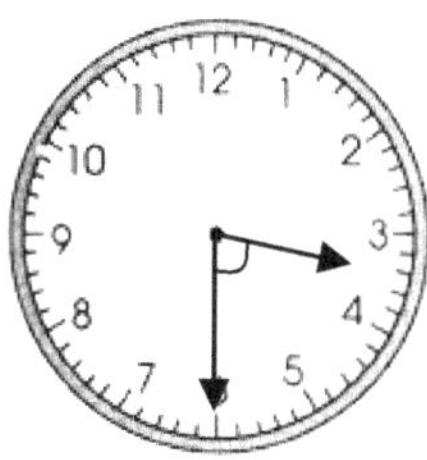

At which of these times is the angle between the hands of the clock the smallest?

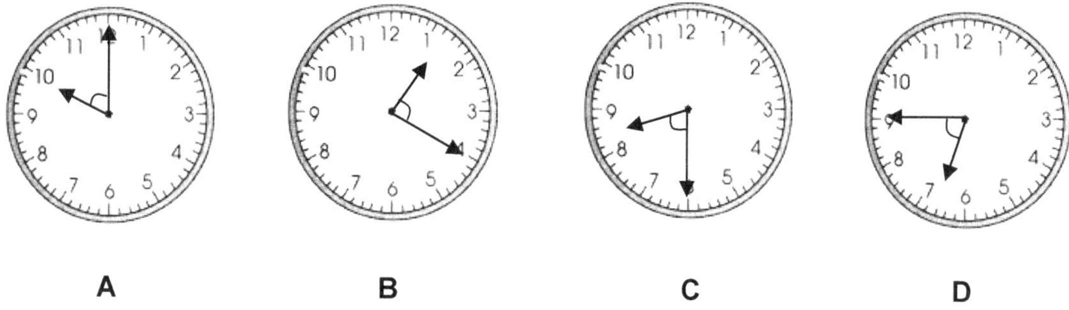

A **B** **C** **D**

5

> To make a working laptop, you need to have good coding skills and an excellent approach on hardware.

Sam: “Sally is extremely good at coding. The only problem is that she does not know much about hardware. Regardless, she will make a working laptop.”

Sally: “Sam has an excellent approach to hardware, however, he does not know much about coding and programming languages. He will certainly make one of the best working laptops.”

If the information in the box is true, whose reasoning is correct?

A Sam Only

B Sally Only

C Both Sam and Sally

D Neither Sam nor Sally

6 Travis, Justin and Laroi are standing in a horizontal line.

If Justin is to the left of Laroi, and Laroi is to the right of Travis, which one of the following must be true?

A Travis is in the middle of the other two

B Laroi is on the furthest right

C Travis is to the furthest right

D Justin is in the middle of the other two

7

Jimmy and Kendell are in a classroom.

Jimmy: "Sally asked me to get her MacBook for her, but I can't seem to find it here. It's a grey coloured MacBook."

Kendell: "Ooh look I see a grey MacBook there. That must be Sally's MacBook."

Which one of the following sentences shows the mistake Kendell has made?

A There are many grey MacBooks, so it might not be Sally's

B Sally must be the one who should come get her MacBook and not make Jimmy do it

C Kendell purposely pointed at the wrong MacBook because she does not like Sally

D Kendell isn't too sure what a MacBook looks like.

8 Four children collected shells on the beach. They put their shells in piles as shown.

Child	Number of shells collected	Number of shells in each pile
Dennis	48	4
Jonathan	72	6
Andrew	65	5
Neil	77	7

Who made the largest number of piles?

A Dennis

B Jonathan

C Andrew

D Neil

9 There are six towns (Barley, Cale, Delhi, Elmo, France, and Guernsey) in a region.

Cale is north of Delhi and northeast of Barley. Delhi is north of Elmo and west of France. Guernsey is east of France.

Which town is northwest of Elmo?

- **A** Barley
- **B** France
- **C** Guernsey
- **D** Delhi

10 Two people saw different views of the same object. The views of each person are given below.

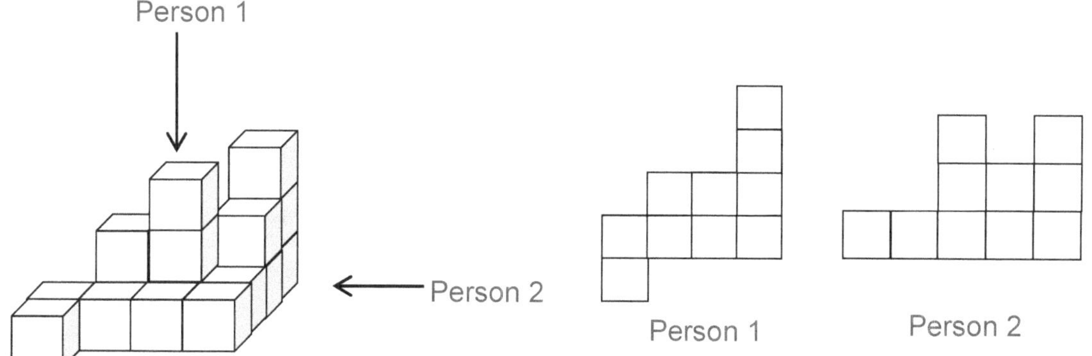

Which statement is correct?

- **A** Both people have the correct view.
- **B** Only person 1's view is correct.
- **C** Neither of them has the correct view.
- **D** Only person 2's view is correct.

11 In a survey of gamers, everyone who liked Burritos liked Burgers. Everyone who liked Burgers liked Pizza, but no one who liked Burgers liked Tacos.

Danny, Alan, Kevin and Lassie all took part in the survey.

Based on the above information, which one of the following must be true?

A If Danny likes Pizzas, he also likes Burgers

B If Alan does not like Tacos, she does not like Pizza

C If Kevin does not like Burritos, he does not like Burgers

D If Jess likes Burritos, she does not like Tacos

12 Sports specialists say that: "All cricket batsman must wear a helmet".

Which one of the statements, if true, best supports the sports specialists' claim?

A Helmets are uncomfortable to wear and look very fashionable

B Helmets decrease the effect the ball may have if hit on the head

C Cricket players may swing the bat onto their heads and get seriously injured

D If you are not a cricket batsman, you don't need a helmet

13 Jenny is writing a letter to her daughter's school board to encourage the canteen to have healthier lunches available for the children instead of junk food.

Which one of the following statements **strengthens** her argument the most?

A Illnesses like the flu and the common cold are very frequent in schools.

B Nearby houses have complained that students are very loud during their breaks.

C Doctors have stated that a good diet for children can help with their attention and focus.

D Students are often very energetic during their breaks.

14 As Ronaldo was learning to play soccer, his coach told him: "To even have the slightest chance to play for Portugal, you must know how to kick the ball into the goal."

If Ronaldo's coach is correct, which one of these statements will be true?

A Everyone who knows how to kick a ball into a goal will play for Portugal.

B If you do not know how to kick a ball into the goal, you can play for any team, besides Portugal

C All players in the Portugal team know how to kick the ball into the goal

D Kicking the ball into the goal is harder than becoming a goalkeeper

15 The pie graph shows the proportion of Australian people in different age groups.

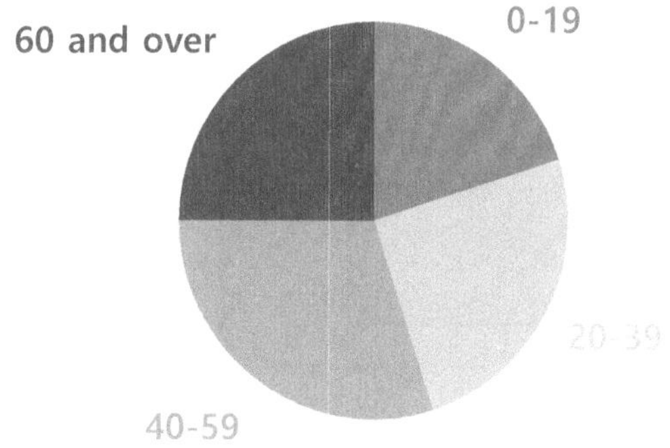

The graph shows that more than half of Australians are aged

A 60 and over.

B 40 and over.

C under 40.

D under 20.

16 Doctors suggest stretching and eating a healthy breakfast every morning.

Which one of the statements, if true, best supports the Doctors' claim?

A This especially applies to people over the age of 18
B This promotes a healthy lifestyle for all people
C This makes sure that children will grow strong and tall
D Eating an apple a day will also help to do this

17 Meg went on a road trip across the desert.

The air conditioning system inside the car was faulty, resulting in the temperature inside the car fluctuating.

If the air conditioning system initially worked but broke down twice, which of the following graphs accurately shows the temperature changes within the car?

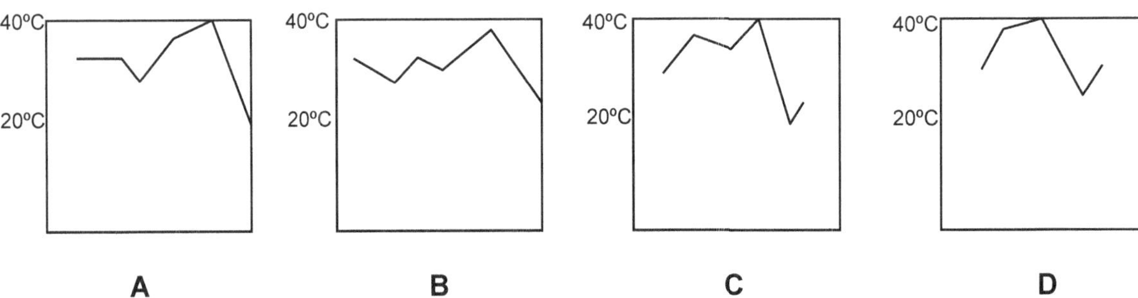

18 Brian, Dom and Vince all have cars. Brian owns a Ferrari, Lamborghini and Toyota. Dom owns a Lamborghini, Nissan and Toyota. Vince owns a Toyota, Subaru and McLaren.

Which cars does Brian or Dom own that Vince does not?

A McLaren, Lamborghini
B Lamborghini, Nissan, Toyota
C Lamborghini, Nissan, Ferrari
D Lamborghini, Nissan, Subaru

19 Harry owns a folder with all of Terry's movies

Harry: "If you tell me the name of a movie, I will tell you when it was released."

Which one of the following sentences shows the mistake Alan has made?

A Terry is not in many movies.
B Movies can change names over time
C There can be more than one movie with the same name
D Terry's movies may not have a name to them

20 Jess wants to make a cube so that the same number is written on opposite faces.

Which of these could be the net of this cube?

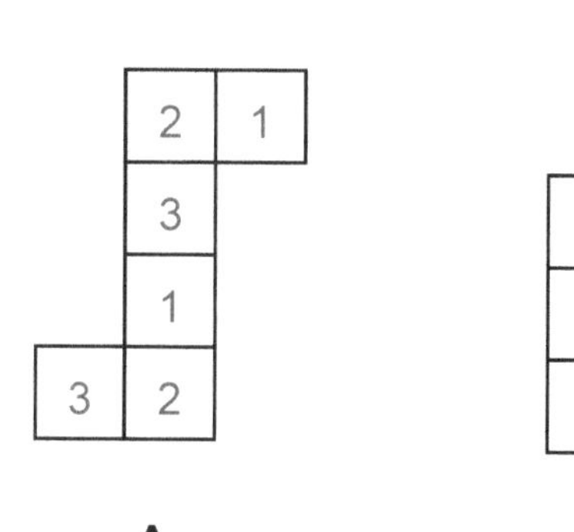

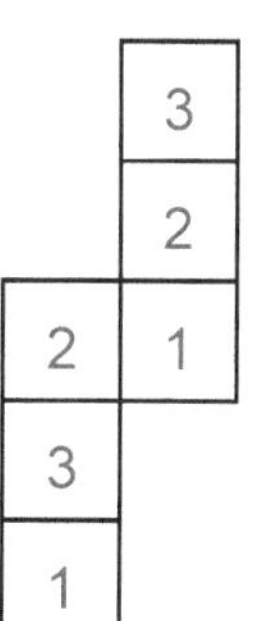

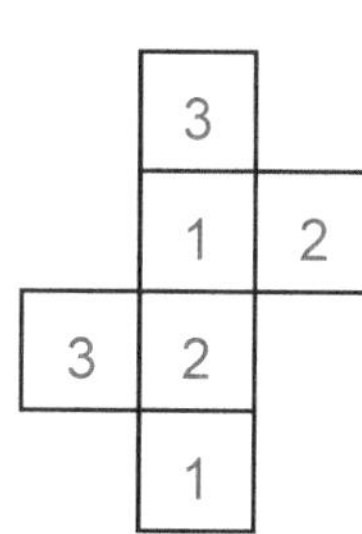

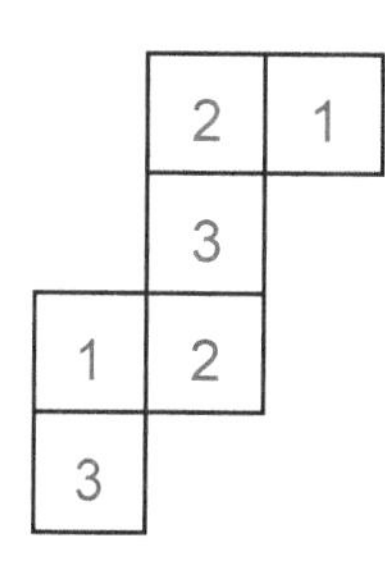

A **B** **C** **D**

21

At the baseball competition, whoever makes the top 5 will be allowed to move into the next round. Additionally, whoever that can prove that their bat was faulty, can proceed to the next round

Louise: "A maximum of 6 people can make it to the next round"

What mistake has Louise made in her statement?

A More than 1 person can prove that their bat was faulty
B We are not told how many people will be in the competition
C Everyone in the top 5 could have had faulty bats
D Some people may not want to participate next round

22 Next year I am buying a new car and I need to choose from 4 cars to pick.

I have to choose one car from each of the following lists.

LIST 1	LIST 2	LIST 3	LIST 4
Nissan	Subaru	Lamborghini	GTI
Supra	Toyota	Yaris	Nissan
Ferrari	R34	Skyline	Supra
GTI	Lamborghini	McLaren	Audi

I know that I want to choose Audi, McLaren and Supra?

Which one of the following can I NOT choose as my final car?

A Nissan

B Lamborghini

C Subaru

D R34

23 Letty, Mia, Jason, and Snoop are seated around a table on a train. 2 of them are facing forwards (in the direction of travel), while the other 2 face backwards. 2 of them have window seats while the other 2 have aisle seats.

I know that:
Letty is sitting diagonally opposite Jason
Snoop is facing forwards
Mia is next to Letty

Which one of the following do I also know?

A Letty is sitting opposite Snoop

B Jason is traveling backwards

C Jason has a window seat

D Mia has an aisle seat

24 The graph shows the average temperature in Perth for one year.

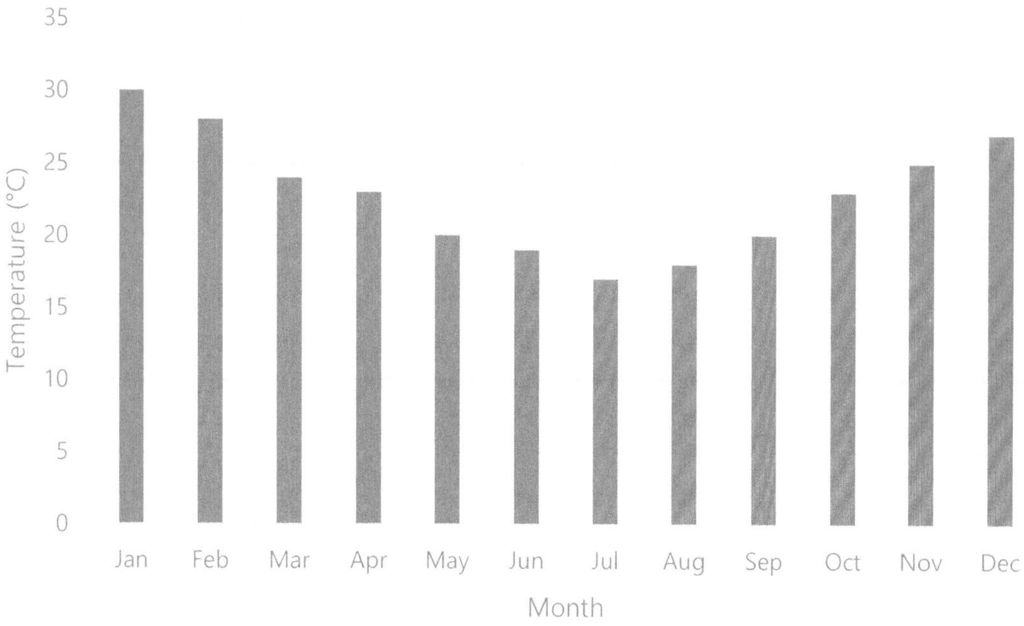

Which of the following statements is true?

A The average temperature in March was greater than in November

B The average temperature in October was greater than in January

C On average, every month was hotter than 15°C

D December was the hottest month on average

25 Sheldon and Leonard were having a talk about their future careers and Sheldon remarked that he was going to give up drawing to focus on becoming a physicist. However, Leonard was very against this. Leonard said, "You don't need to give up drawing just because you want to work on becoming a physicist."

Which one of the statements, if true, most **strengthens** Leonard's argument?

A Drawing is sometimes an essential part when it comes to physics and maths

B Knowing how to draw gives you a boost upon other physicists and can help you become famous

C Drawing is beneficial in case Sheldon cannot become a physicist and wants to become an artist

D Leonard is good at drawing and can help Sheldon out

26 You can only go on the ride if you are more than 130cm tall and do not get sick easily

If this is true, which one of the sentences must also be true?

A If Jack was 130cm tall and was brave, he could go on the ride

B Adam can go on the ride because he was 135cm tall and does not get sick easily

C If Alex could not go on the ride, it is because he was 140cm tall

D Rides are only allowed with a ticket

27 Alan, Brenda, Kalie and Darren play in a sports team. The coach said that "If Alan does not play tomorrow, then Brenda will start on and play. If Alan plays, then Kalie will replace Darren and play."

If Brenda does not play tomorrow, which of the other 3 will be on the team?

A Kalie Only

B Alan Only

C Darren only

D Alan and Kalie

28 **Ninja**: "To be able to build fast in Fortnite, you must have all the keys memorised on your keyboard"

PewDiePie: "I know all the keys on the keyboard, which means I will be able to build fast in Fortnite"

Which one of these sentences shows the mistake PewDiePie has made?

A Ninja's keyboard could be different from PewDiePie's, meaning that he doesn't need to memorise the keyboard

B Just because you know all the keys doesn't mean you memorized them

C Fortnite can be played on a PlayStation so you don't need a keyboard

D PewDiePie hasn't practiced as much as Ninja

29 A goal post consists of 3 bars. The right bar, the left bar, and the crossbar. Ron kicks a ball towards a goal post while blindfolded and hears a noise of the ball hitting one of the bars.

Which of the statements must be true?

A The goal keeper might've accidentally hit the goal post

B The ball must have hit the crossbar

C If the ball did not hit the cross bar, it must have hit the right or left bar

D The ball must have bounced on the ground and hit either one of the bars

30 In a sprint with 4 people, Corey is 4 m behind Larry, and 9 m ahead of Ryan.

If Daniel is 16m ahead of Ryan, who is in second place?

A Corey

B Larry

C Ryan

D Daniel

OC Practice Test Paper

Thinking Skills 7 (Time allowed: 30 min)

INSTRUCTIONS

1 Write your Name on the cover page.

2 There are **30** questions in this paper. For each question there are four possible answers, **A**, **B**, **C** and **D**. Choose the **one** correct answer and record your choice on the separate answer sheet. If you make a mistake, erase thoroughly and try again.

3 You will **not** lose marks for incorrect answers, so you should attempt **all 30** questions

4 You **must** complete the answer sheet within the time limit. There will **not** be any extra time at the end of the exam to record your answers on the answer sheet.

5 You can use the question paper for working out, but no extra paper is allowed.

6 Calculators and dictionaries are **NOT** allowed.

Name: ______________________________

1 Which set of properties is true for a pentagonal pyramid?

	Edges	Faces	Vertices
A	10	6	6
B	8	5	5
C	6	6	6
D	5	5	5

2 Andy, Simon, Emma and Holly are seated around the dinner table. Two of them are facing towards the kitchen and two of them are facing towards the living room (the back of the house).

I know that:

- Andy is sitting diagonally opposite Emma
- Holly is facing the kitchen
- Simon is next to Andy

Which of the following is an assumption that can be made?

A Emma is facing the living room

B Holly is sitting opposite Emma

C Simon is closest to the door

D Andy is sitting opposite Holly

3 A scientist claims: “Global warming is a rising issue that threatens not just our environment, but the survival of its inhabitants.”

Which one of these statements, if true, best supports the scientist’s claim?

A Global warming is only a minor issue

B The effects of global warming are not always felt

C If global warming is not addressed, eventually all life may die out

D The issue of global warming is being addressed and change is happening to protect our earth

4

> When a student gets called into the Deputy Principal's office, it is either because they are in trouble, of if the Deputy Principal needs to collect a form from the student.

Jeremy: "I was called into the Deputy Principal's office, which means I am in trouble."

Ria: "No Jeremy, there could be another reason why you got called."

If the information in the box is true, whose reasoning is correct?

A Jeremy only
B Ria only
C Both Jeremy and Ria
D Neither Jeremy nor Ria

5 These are three views of the same cube.

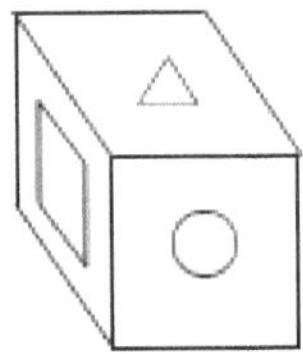
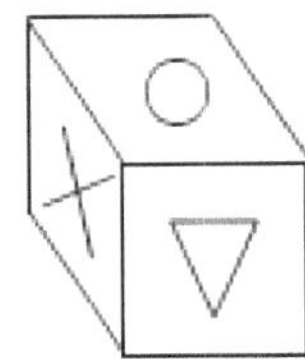
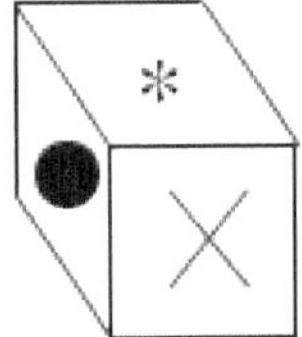

Which is the correct net for this cube?

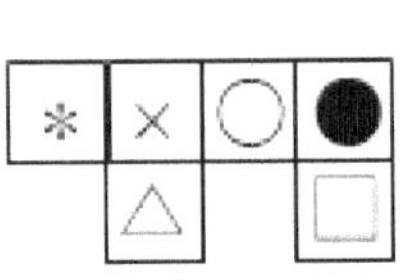
A

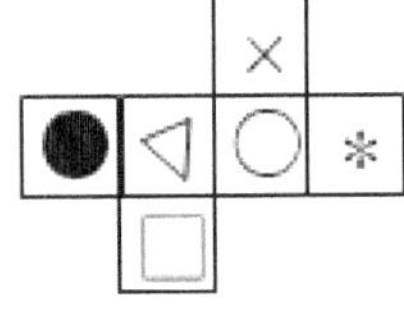
B

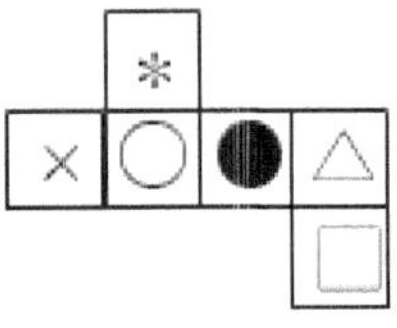
C

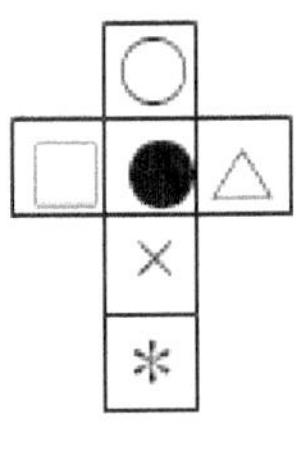
D

6 To be in primary school, you must be aged 13 or below.

Students go straight from primary to high school.

All sixteen-year-old individuals are high school students.

Some high school students are in the chess club.

Lily is a fifteen-year-old individual.

Which of the following statements is true?

A Lily is a high school student
B Lily is in the chess club
C All students in the chess club are friends with Lily
D Chess club is the most popular club in the school

7 **Jo**: "If you would like to find a job after university, you must apply to lots of jobs."

Which of the following sentences shows the mistake Jo has made?

A Applying for jobs can be very stressful
B You may be able to find a job without applying for multiple jobs
C Applying to jobs will take up too much time and only make you stressed
D B and C

8 Five friends are given one card, each with a number 1,2,3,4 or 5. Each friend has a different favourite colour.

- Those with even numbers do not like any of the primary colours
- Joseph's favourite colour is green and his number is 2
- Daisy's favourite colour is blue
- Jennifer has the number 5
- Adolf has the number 1
- Poppy has an even number

Using the information above, find Daisy's number.

A 4
B 1
C 3
D 5

9 Choose the shape that joins with the following to form a square.

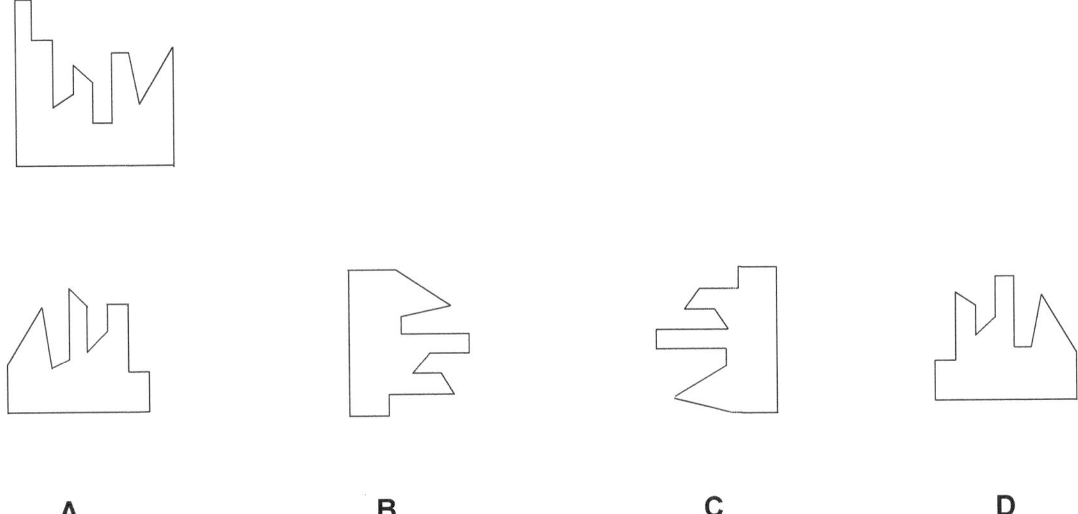

10 A health expert once said during the coronavirus pandemic: “The more that people wear masks and maintain good hygiene, the less the coronavirus will spread.”

Which of the following statements, if true, best supports the health expert’s claim?

A Good hygiene does not mean the coronavirus will not enter the body.

B The less the coronavirus spreads, the quicker this pandemic will be over.

C Masks may not prevent the coronavirus from entering the body.

D Following the guidelines above will guarantee that individuals will not get coronavirus.

11 The table shows how long four students took to run a 100m race and a 400m race at a sports event.

Name	Time to complete 100m race (seconds)	Time to complete 400m race (seconds)
Jonathan	12.9	69.7
Dennis	13.7	71.8
Andrew	15.1	59.2
Neil	14.6	64.9

Which student took less than 15 seconds to complete the 100m race and less than 65 seconds to complete the 400m race?

A Jonathan

B Dennis

C Andrew

D Neil

12

> Whenever the school gives us ice-blocks, it means that they have extra money to spend on students. And whenever they give us ice-blocks, students always get free time.

Daniel: "I was away but my friend told me you guys got free time yesterday. That must mean the school had extra money to spend on the students."

Josh: "The school is always so greedy."

If the information in the box is true, whose reasoning is correct?

A Daniel only

B Josh only

C Both Daniel and Josh

D Neither Daniel nor Josh

13 Choose the side view of this figure.

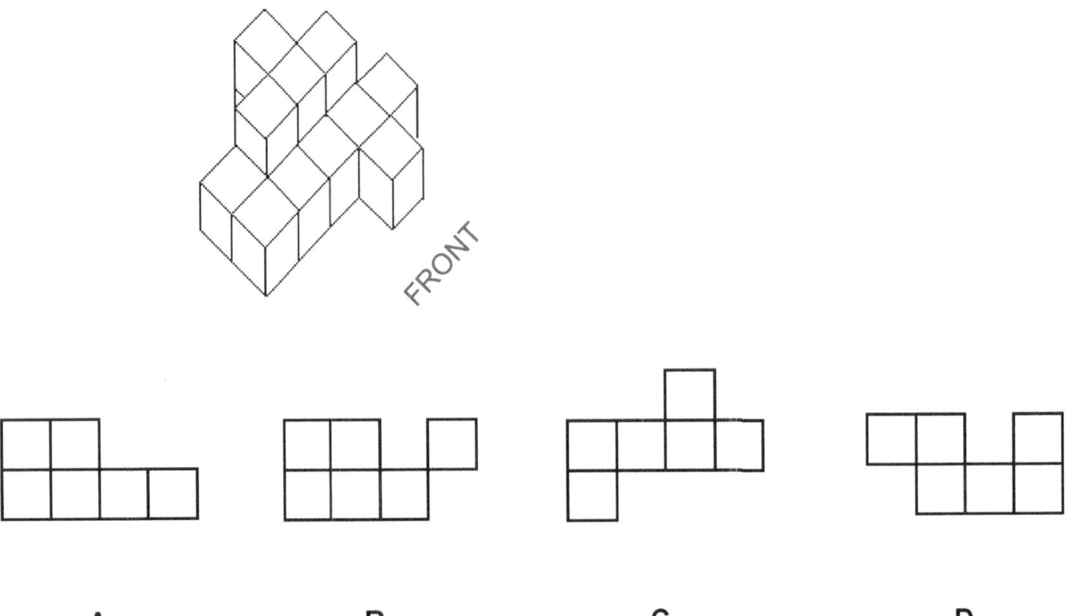

A **B** **C** **D**

14 All musicians play instruments.

All oboe players are musicians.

Oboes and pianos are instruments.

Frankie is a musician.

Which statement is true?

A All musicians are oboe players
B All musicians are piano or oboe players
C Frankie is an oboe player
D None of the above

15 A teacher is trying to arrange the 5 students in her class into a seating plan.

There are 2 tables in the room and each of them can seat 3 people.

We also know that:

- The tables are arranged 1 behind the other
- Ashley must sit on the front row on the left-hand side because she has poor eyesight
- Bella must sit in the middle on the front row and Caitlin cannot sit on the same row as Bella
- Danielle needs to sit next to an empty seat as she sometimes has help from a teaching assistant
- Emily has to sit at the end of a row because it is hard for her to get into a middle seat

Using the information above, find out who is sitting in the front right seat.

A Emily

B Bella

C Caitlin

D Danielle

16 I am sitting in an assembly room with the seats arranged in a rectangle.

There are 48 of us in total, and we will up all the seats.

If I'm sitting in the second last row and there are 3 people to my left and 2 people to my right, how many rows are there in front of me?

A 7

B 4

C 5

D 6

17 Dentists recommend that brushing teeth twice and flossing once daily should be used to maintain good oral hygiene, which improves their dental health, and there are studies to support this claim.

Which one of these statements, if true, best supports the claim made by dentists?

A Brushing teeth too often can lead to bleeding gums

B Brushing may not prevent some dental diseases

C Brushing teeth regularly can prevent cavities by 60%

D Brushing teeth once daily is sufficient to prevent many diseases

18 The table shows the number of steaks sold for lunch at a bar each day last week.

Day of Week	Number of Steaks
Saturday	42
Sunday	21
Monday	30
Tuesday	57
Wednesday	31
Thursday	21
Friday	44

Which statement is correct according to the data?

A The number of orders on Saturday was higher than Sunday and Thursday combined

B Tuesday has more orders than Sunday and Monday combined

C Monday had the highest number of orders.

D The number of orders on the weekend equals the number or orders on the weekdays

19 Mia, Jamie and John all have different tastes in food. Mia likes cookies, fish, soup, pizza and muffins. Jamie likes ice-cream, muffins and pizza. John likes fish, pie, pizza, pasta and muffins.

Which foods does Mia like that neither Jamie nor John like?

A Fish and cookies

B Soup and pizza

C Pasta and ice-cream

D Cookies and soup

20 Lisa needs to choose 4 extra-curricular activities to pursue in her spare time.

She must choose one activity from each of the following lists:

List 1	**List 2**	**List 3**	**List 4**
Painting	Ice-skating	Ice-skating	Swimming
Knitting	Trumpet	Knitting	Flute
Piano	Basketball	Flute	Volunteering
Volunteering	Violin	Drums	Maths lessons

She knows she definitely, wants to do ice-skating, piano and flute lessons.

Which one of the following can she **NOT** choose as her final activity?

A Painting

B Knitting

C Violin

D Volunteering

21 The numbers of different colours of cars sold on Christmas Island are given in the following table.

Colour	Red	White	Black	Silver
Number of cars sold	10	20	20	50

Which of the following pie charts could represent this data?

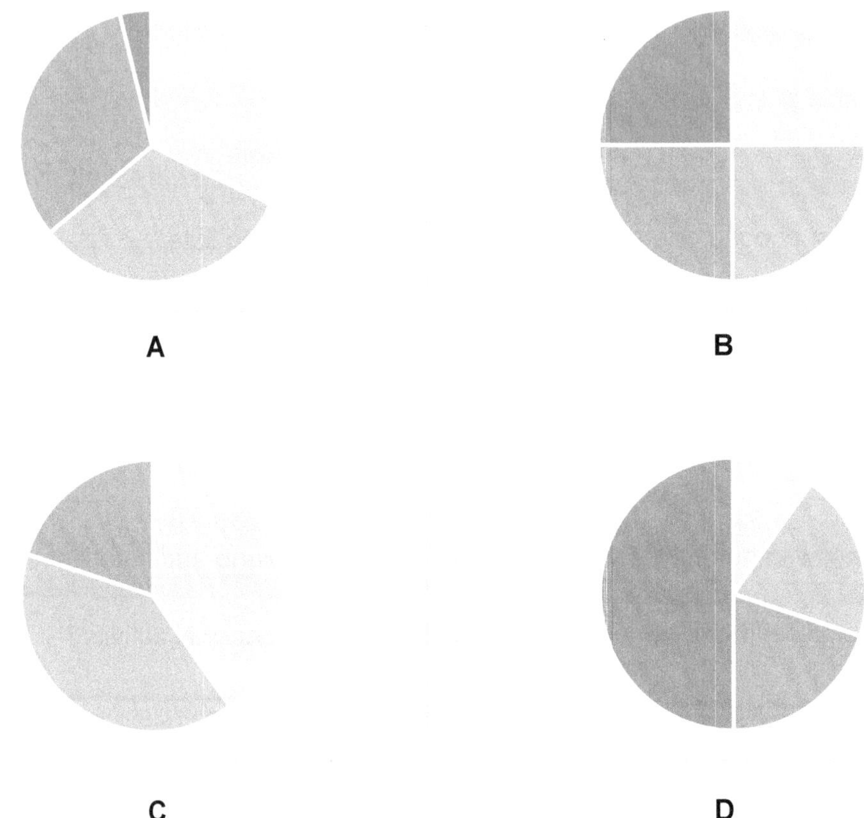

22 This label on a coat in a clothes store caught my attention.

Three of the four figures were correct, while one of them was a mistake.

Which one of the four figures on the label was the mistake?

A 10

B 20

C 30

D 40

23

In a week, a school will be running a carnival. Students will only be allowed to attend the carnival if they have returned their signed permission notes.

Jason: “Andre said he will be handing in his note tomorrow which means he will definitely be allowed to go to the carnival.”

Luke: “Tony is currently on holiday. He will not be here for this whole week for him to hand in his note. This means he cannot go to the carnival.”

If the information in the box is true, whose reasoning is correct?

A Jason only

B Luke only

C Both Jason and Luke

D Neither Jason nor Luke

24 Amy, Rishi and Bethany stand in a line. Amy is in front of Rishi and Bethany is behind Amy.

Which one of the following statements must be true?

A Rishi is at the very front of the line
B Bethany is at the very back of the line
C Amy is in the middle of the line
D Amy is at the very front of the line

25 John and Nicky have a conversation:

John: "I am helping my mum look for her mobile phone. It has a black colour."

Nicky: "I saw a black mobile phone in the lost property collection. It must be hers!"

Which one of the following sentences shows the mistake Nicky has made?

A John's mum might have found her phone
B The phone Nicky saw may have belonged to someone else
C Someone may have stolen John's mum's phone
D The phone case may have been removed

26 A teacher says: "All students wishing to get a mark above 90 must do lots of questions from the textbook."

Which one of these statements, if true, best supports the teacher's claim?

A You are more likely to score above 90 if you do questions from the textbook
B Those students who achieved 80 did the questions from the textbook
C Textbook questions are more helpful than just simply reading notes
D Textbook questions are made better now than before

27 When Mila mentioned she wanted to enter the drawing competition, her art teacher at school advised her: "To even have a chance of placing in the competition, you must have used lots of colours and made your drawing look realistic."

If Mila's art teacher is correct, which one of these statements will be true?

A All of the participants of this competition who will have used lots of colours in their works will definitely win

B Participants who do not use lots of colours will not win the competition

C Some of the participants who did not use lots of colours will place

D Only those who use lots of colours will place in the competition

28 On sports day at Sydney Academy points are awarded in each event as follows:

winner	10 points
2nd place	5 points
3rd place	3 points
4th place	1 point

Each student may enter no more than two events.

What are the total points that it is **not** possible for an individual student to score?

A 4

B 8

C 16

D 20

29

> Parrots are the only birds with bright red and green feathers, are very loud and can measure up to 25 cm long.

Sasha: "This bird has bright red and green feathers, so it must be a parrot."

Alex: "But it is only 10 cm long, so it cannot be a parrot."

If the information in the box is true, whose reasoning is correct?

A Sasha only

B Alex only

C Both Sasha and Alex

D Neither Sasha nor Alex

30 **Sandy**: "I know that there are exactly 30 students in this class but only 20 are here today. This must mean that 10 people are sick today."

Which statement best represents the mistake that Sandy has made?

A Sandy did not mention that some students may not be in her class

B She did not say which students are sick

C The other children could be absent for different reasons

D Sandy may have counted wrong

OC Practice Test Paper

Thinking Skills 8 (Time allowed: 30 min)

INSTRUCTIONS

1 Write your Name on the cover page.

2 There are **30** questions in this paper. For each question there are four possible answers, **A**, **B**, **C** and **D**. Choose the **one** correct answer and record your choice on the separate answer sheet. If you make a mistake, erase thoroughly and try again.

3 You will **not** lose marks for incorrect answers, so you should attempt **all 30** questions

4 You **must** complete the answer sheet within the time limit. There will **not** be any extra time at the end of the exam to record your answers on the answer sheet.

5 You can use the question paper for working out, but no extra paper is allowed.

6 Calculators and dictionaries are **NOT** allowed.

Name: ______________________________

1 A music teacher has suggested that learning how to play instruments should be an important part of school life, and that school children should spend as much time learning instruments as they do playing sports.

Which one of these statements, if true, best supports the music teacher's claim?

A Instruments are expensive and require a lot of effort

B Some students do not like playing instruments because it's boring

C Music helps in maintaining a healthy mindset

D Schools do not have enough qualified music teachers

2 200 people were interviewed and asked their opinion about redeveloping the railway station.

Unfortunately, when a journalist received the data for publication, some data were missing. The table he received is shown below.

Gender	*For*	*Against*	*Unsure*
Male	65		35
Female	55	16	25
Total	**120**		

How many people in total voted against the development?

A 35

B 30

C 25

D 20

3 Josh, Eve and Kyle all keep different branded clothes. Josh has Nike, Puma and Fila. Eve has Puma, Fila and Adidas. Kyle has Champion, New Balance and Gucci.

Which branded clothes does Josh keep that neither Eve nor Kyle keeps?

A Puma and Nike

B Nike

C Fila and Nike

D Gucci

4 Only those students who return their notes at the meeting at recess today will be allowed to go on the excursion next week.

Bryce: "Taylor is sick today, however as he returned his note last week he will still be able to go"

Taylor: "Bryce's brother gave his note in for him so he must be going on the excursion"

If the information in the box is true, whose reasoning is correct?

- **A** Bryce only
- **B** Taylor only
- **C** Both Bryce and Taylor
- **D** Neither Bruce nor Taylor

5 The table shows how much money was raised from different activities at a school fair.

Activity	Money Raised ($)
Cake stall	50
Book stall	65
Face painting	33
Toy sale	45
Food stall	25
Sack race	13

Which column on the graph shows the amount of money raised from Toy sale?

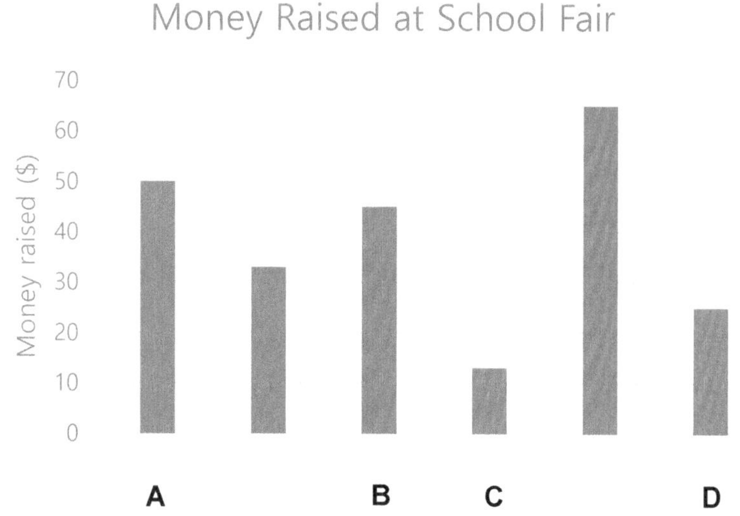

6 Josh, Noah and Blake are standing in a row.

If Josh is to the right of Noah and Blake is to the right of Josh, which one of the following statements must be true?

A Noah is furthest to the right
B Blake is furthest to the left
C Josh is furthest to the right
D Josh is in the middle

7 Sam and Josh are sitting in their classroom.

Sam: "Katy asked me to get her bag, but I can't seem to find it here. It's black with a green badge, she says".

Josh: "Here's a black bag with a green badge – it must be hers!"

Which one of the following sentences shows the mistake Josh has made?

A Even if the bag is black, it might not have a green badge
B There might be more than one black bag with a green badge
C Josh might be looking for the wrong bag as he may not know which specific green coloured badge
D Katy might have another one

8 Transport NSW says: "Anyone on public transport should wear a mask"

Which one of these statements, if true, best supports the above claim?

A Those that wear masks are less likely to contract a disease or illness
B By wearing masks, the government is able to increase their mask revenue
C People on trains are more likely to fall down
D Masks assist in covering faces and hiding from police

9 Alan drew this shape.

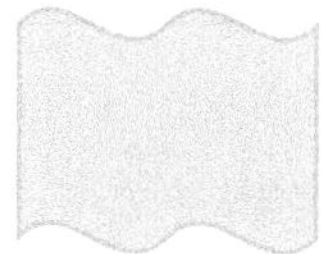

Which of these shows Alan's shape flipped and turned?

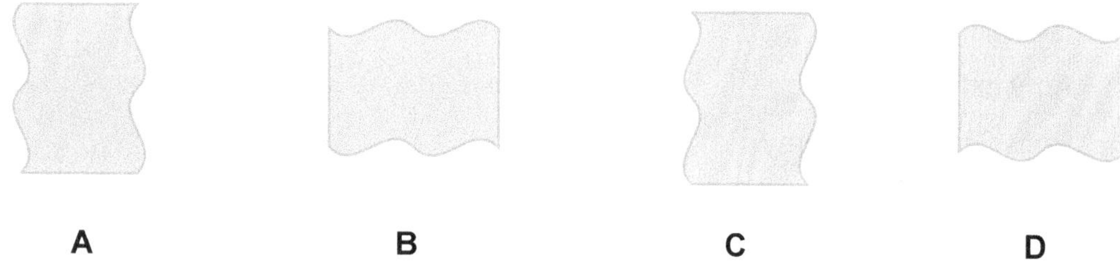

A **B** **C** **D**

10 When Joseph was studying for the end of term exam, his teacher told him: "To have even a chance of getting a distinction in the exam you must have completed 10 practice papers".

If Joseph's instructor is correct, which one of these statements will be true?

A All the students who had completed 10 or more practice papers will definitely get distinctions in the exam

B Some of the students who completed less than 10 hours will still get distinctions in the exam

C Only the students who practised more than 30 hours will pass their test

D No one who completed less than 10 practice papers received distinctions

11

> A cricket bat is grey, with stickers in the middle, and can be bought in 10 different countries. Baseball bats are sold in more countries.

George: "This bat is grey and has stickers, it must be a cricket bat."

Amy: "Yeah, because it's sold in 15 countries so it must be"

If the information in the box is correct, whose reasoning is correct?

A George only
B Amy only
C Both George and Amy
D Neither George nor Amy

12 Identify the shape by using the following clues.

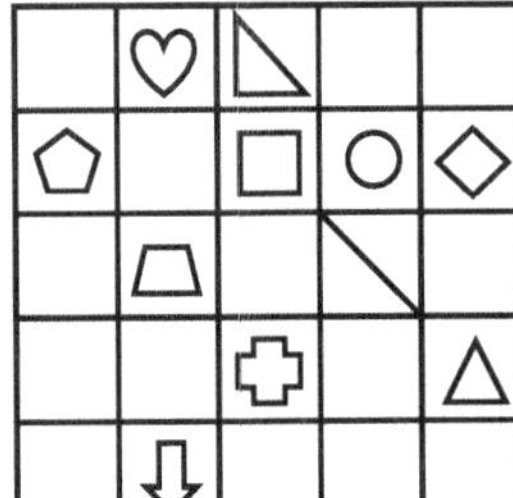

1. Diagonally above ⧅
2. Above ✚
3. Right of ⬠
4. Is in the third column

A ◺
B ○
C ♡
D □

13 **Mr Andrews:** "I know that 10 students in my class have sports today, but I only saw 8 wearing sports shoes this morning. The other two students must be away today.

Which one of the following sentences shows the mistake Mr Andrews has made?

A He did not specify which students he was referring to
B Some of the students might not be wearing sports shoes today
C Some of the students were not present during roll call
D Some of the students did not want to go to sport

14 Josh, Stella, Macy and Dax are seated around a table on a bus.

Two of them are facing forwards (in the direction of travel) and two are facing backwards.

Two have window seats and the other two have aisle seats.

I know that:
Stella is next to Josh;
Dax is facing forward;
Josh is sitting diagonally opposite Macy.

Which one of the following do I also know?

A Macy has a window seat

B Macy is travelling backwards

C Josh is sitting opposite Dax

D Stella has an aisle seat

15 An environmentalist says: "Carbon pollution in our atmosphere is not just a problem for the animals that live here, it affects us too".

Which one of these statements, if true, best supports the environmentalists claim?

A Carbon pollution is not significant enough to have an impact

B We breathe in the same polluted air as animals

C The carbon rises towards the clouds where we don't breathe in that air

D There is plenty of fresh air

16 Which shape has not been used to construct this 2D figure? (The shapes are only representative and are not drawn to scale.)

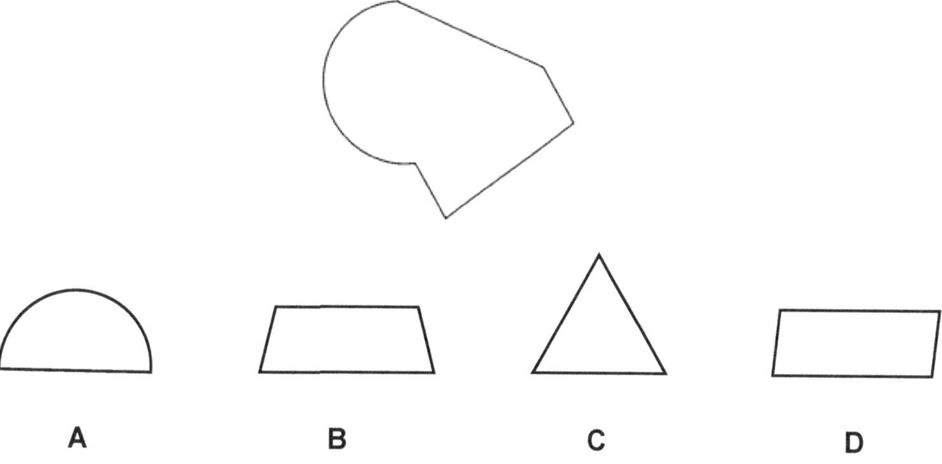

17 Nate, Faran, Steve and David are all part of the local dance squad.

The coach has just told them "If Nate does not dance tomorrow, then Faran will. If Nate does dance, then Steve dance in the place of David"

So if Faran does not dance tomorrow, which of the other three will be on the team?

A Nate only

B Nate and Steve

C Faran and David

D Faran and Nate

18 Vivian wants to purchase 3 pencils for school.

There are 3 stores from which she can buy the pencils and which have special offers.

Store	Standard price	Special offers
Shop 1	$4	Buy one get one half off
Shop 2	$4	Buy one get one free
Shop 3	$3	Buy two get the third free
Shop 4	$3	No special offer

From which store would the pencils be the cheapest?

A Shop 1

B Shop 2

C Shop 3

D Shop 4

19 **Amy:** "To have any chance of passing your driving test, you will need to practice for at least two hours, five times a week".

Scot: "I practice every day for an hour, so I'm sure to pass the exam"

Which one of these sentences shows the mistake Scot has made?

A Taking an exam can be a stressful experience

B Practising every day does not guarantee success in the exam

C Having an experienced co-driver is critical as they are highly influential

D Depending on each car, the recommended practice time varies

20 There are six towns (U, V, W, X, Y and Z) in a region.

Town V is north of Town W and northeast of Town Z. Town W is north of Town X and west of Town Y. Town A is east of Town Y.

Which town is northwest of Town X?

A Town V
B Town W
C Town Y
D Town Z

21 The Simpsons parked in a car lot while they went to the picnic.

How much did they have to pay if they parked from 11:00am until 3:30pm?

PARK YOUR CAR	
	Rates
First hour	$3.00
Each additional hour or part of an hour	$0.50
Maximum	$5.00

A $5.00
B $5.50
C $6.00
D $4.50

22 A nutrionist claimed: "The more water children drink, the better it is for their health".

Which one of these statements, if true, best supports the nutrionist's claim?

A Water helps remove harmful toxins and other substances from the body
B Water is cheap and should therefore be everyone's favourite drink
C By not drinking water, children are able to drink their favourite drinks
D Drinking water leads to excessive use of the toilet

23 Below are three views of the same cube. Which of the four is also the view of this cube?

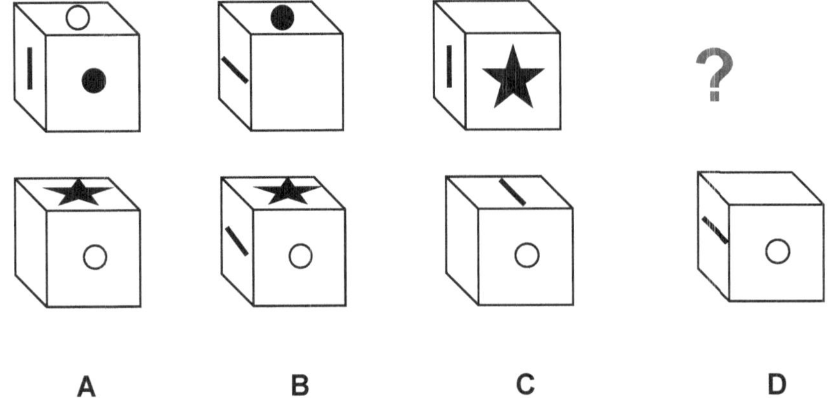

24

Whenever it rains, Mrs Leah always brings an umbrella to school. And when she brings an umbrella, she always gives us free time for an hour.

Sam: "We got free time yesterday – it must have rained"

Joel: "If it rains next week, we are sure to get more free time"

If the information in the box is true, whose reasoning is correct?

A Sam only
B Joel only
C Both Sam and Joel
D Neither Sam nor Joel

25 A health specialist has suggested that PDHPE lessons should be an important part of school life, and that they should be integrated into primary schools in order to educate children from the beginning of puberty.

Which one of these statements, if true, best supports the health specialist's claim?

A Early PDHPE education decreases the risk of children unintentionally harming themselves
B Children already have too much to learn, another subject will just make it harder
C PDHPE is unnecessary for primary school children
D Parents don't want their kids learning about PDHPE in primary school

26 Parth, Kabir and Kylie all keep pets.

Parth has dogs, birds, rats and snakes.

Kabir has cats, snakes and lizards.

Kylie has frogs, insects and dogs.

Which pets does Parth keep that neither Kabir nor Kylie keep?

A dogs and birds
B rats and birds
C birds only
D birds and frogs

27 From a large bag of marbles, Jessie has more marbles than Tom, and Tom has twice as many marbles as Jenna. If June has 6 times more marbles than Jenna, which of the following is true?

A June has 12 times more marbles than Jenna
B Tom has less marbles than Jenna
C Jessie has more than two times marbles than Jenna
D June has 4 times as many marbles as Tom

28 If Kevin does not eat well, then he's likely to be lethargic.

If he is feeling lethargic, then he will not be able to perform to his highest ability at the talent show.

If he performs well at the talent show, then he might win first prize. Otherwise, he does not stand a chance.

If the above statements are correct, which one of the following is **not** possible?

A Kevin did not eat well but still won first prize
B Kevin was lethargic at the talent show but still won first prize
C Kieran performed very well in his talent show but did not win first prize
D Kieran ate well but did not win first prize

29 In order to be a successful architect, you need to think outside the box and have excellent attention to detail.

Josh: "Pat is creative, however, can easily make silly mistakes. Therefore, he can still become a successful architect as his dad will teach him."

Pat: "Josh's laser focus allows him to eliminate the possibility of any mistakes. Therefore, he will become a successful architect."

If the information in the box is true, whose reasoning is correct?

A Josh only
B Pat only
C Both Josh and Pat
D Neither Josh nor Pat

30 "In order to finish their homework, a student requires both knowledge and time"

If this is true, which one of these sentences must also be true?

A If Amy had both knowledge and time, she must have finished her homework
B If Amy finished her homework, she must have copied the answers
C If Amy did not have time, she could not have finished her homework
D If Amy did not have the knowledge nor the time, it was still possible for her to finish her homework

OC Practice Test Paper

Thinking Skills 9 (Time allowed: 30 min)

INSTRUCTIONS

1 Write your Name on the cover page.

2 There are **30** questions in this paper. For each question there are four possible answers, **A**, **B**, **C** and **D**. Choose the **one** correct answer and record your choice on the separate answer sheet. If you make a mistake, erase thoroughly and try again.

3 You will **not** lose marks for incorrect answers, so you should attempt **all 30** questions

4 You **must** complete the answer sheet within the time limit. There will **not** be any extra time at the end of the exam to record your answers on the answer sheet.

5 You can use the question paper for working out, but no extra paper is allowed.

6 Calculators and dictionaries are **NOT** allowed.

Name: ______________________________

1 Kimmy's class can choose what colour they want their next folders to be.

They could vote to have purple, green or black folders.

Everyone could only choose one colour and the colour would only be chosen if everyone chose the same colour.

Knowing **one** of the following would allow us to know the result of the vote. Which one is it?

A Only three people voted for black
B No one voted for green or purple
C Everyone voted for green or black
D Black was the most popular vote

2 Dennis is facing north and Andrew is facing south.

Dennis makes a quarter turn to his right, while Andrew makes a quarter turn to his left.

Which statement is TRUE?

A Dennis is now facing west.
B They are facing the same direction.
C Dennis is facing the opposite direction from Andrew.
D Andrew is a quarter turn to the right of Dennis.

3 Kris believes that gyms should lower the minimum age needed to obtain a membership.

Which one of these statements, if true, best supports the Kris' idea?

A Some young people should not be at the gym unsupervised
B The gym has a lot of heavy equipment that can be dangerous
C Some young people will hurt themselves at the gym
D This will result in more younger people maintaining their health

4 Harry, Idris and Jack all have different flavours of ice cream in their fridges.

Harry has chocolate, mint, strawberry and vanilla.

Idris has cookies, vanilla and strawberry.

Jack has honey, strawberry, rocky road and vanilla.

Which ice cream does Harry have that neither Idris **nor** Jack has?

A Vanilla and honey
B Strawberry and mint
C Chocolate and mint
D Mint and rocky road

5 A paper square has been folded into quarters and shapes are cut out.

When opened it looks like this.

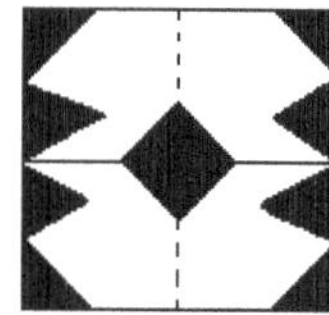

Choose the folded paper which shows how the paper was cut.

A

B

C

D

6 Cadie, Catherine, Charles and Chris are on the Cheerleading team.

The Cheerleading coach has announced that: "If Cadie does not perform tomorrow, then Catherine will perform. If Cadie does perform then Charles will take Chris' place".

So, if Catherine does not perform tomorrow, which of the other three cheerleaders will be at practice?

A Charles and Chris

B Cadie and Charles

C Catherine only

D Charles only

7 Jessie thinks free knee pads should be available at the skate park.

Which one of the following statements, if true, best supports Jessie's idea?

A Knee pads are uncomfortable for skaters

B Knee pads would not be needed for professionals

C It would be very expensive for the skate park to buy kneepads

D This would mean there are less injuries that occur

8

Whenever Penelope's teacher does not get her classroom cleaned on the weekends, she gets angry. And when she gets angry, she yells at her class a lot

Penelope: "My teacher yelled at our class a lot today, she must not have had her classroom cleaned on the weekend".

Penelope's friend: "Yeah that is the only reason why your teacher would be yelling a lot".

If the information in the box is true, whose reasoning is correct?

A Penelope only

B Penelope's friend only

C Both Penelope and her friend

D Neither Penelope nor her friend

9 Vivian grouped all the students in his class by their hair colour.

The graph shows the number of students in each group.

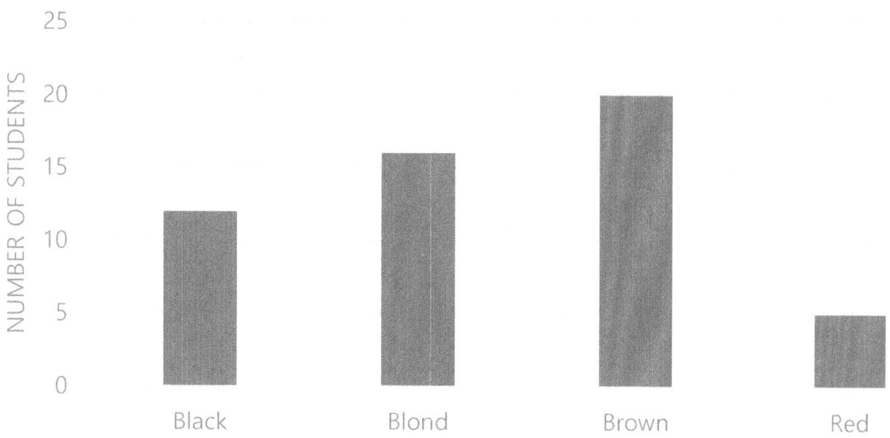

How many students are in Vivian's class?

A 34

B 40

C 48

D 53

10 At the end of the term, I have to choose what electives I want to do for the next term.

I have to choose one subject from each of the following lists:

List 1:	**List 2:**	**List 3:**	**List 4:**
History	Commerce	Commerce	Food Technology
Fashion	Food technology	Fashion	Art
Photography	Sport	Art	Drama
Drama	Textiles	Software design	Software design

I know I want to do commerce, photography and art.

Which of the following can I **not** choose as my final subject?

A History

B Photograph

C Art

D Food Technology

11 There are many different nets of a cube.

Which of these will **not** fold to make a cube?

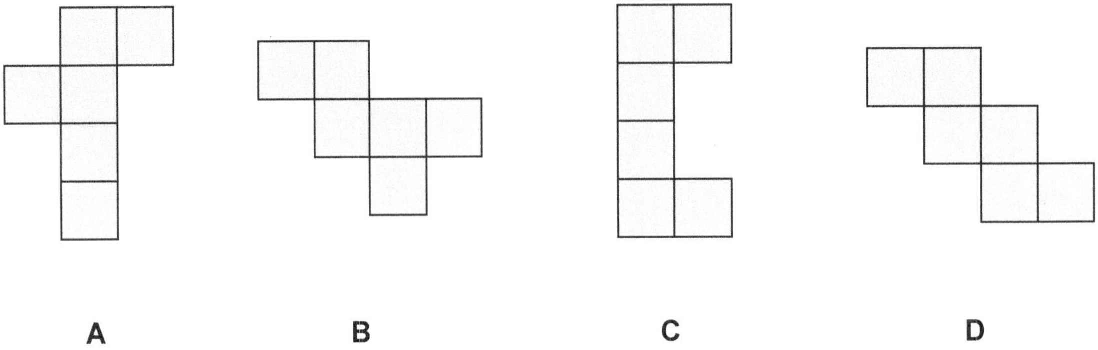

A **B** **C** **D**

12

> Only people that have done the minimum volunteer requirements will be allowed to enjoy the free food buffet at the end of the term. If they haven't done so, they must pay an admissions fee of $4.

Ben: "Jessie was allowed to eat at the end of term buffet, this means she must have met the minimum volunteer requirements for the term".

Claire: "No, she might have paid the admissions fee".

If the information in the box above is true, whose reasoning is correct?

A Ben only
B Claire only
C Both Ben and Claire
D Neither Ben nor Claire

13 Dylan, Elle and Frank are standing in the front row of the street dance performance.

If Dylan is to the right of Elle and Frank is to the left of Dylan, which one of the following statements must be true?

A Elle is furthest to the right
B Dylan is in the middle
C Frank is the furthest to the left
D Dylan is furthest to the right

14 Choose the top view of this figure.

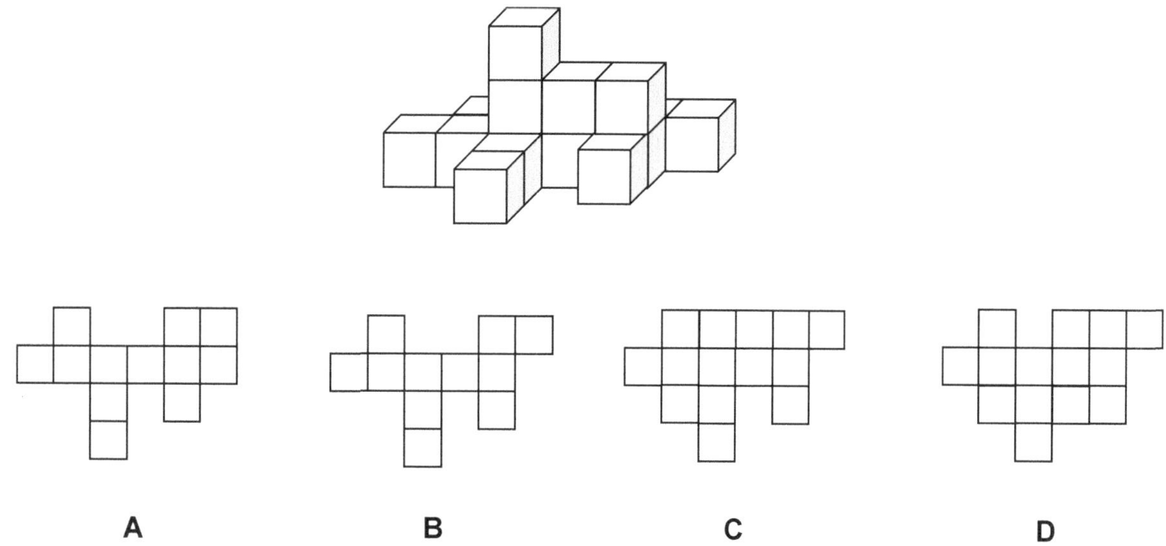

15

Dan and Tara are at the train station.

Dan: "The only train we can catch is on the T2 railway line and normally those trains are older so they have less seats".

Tara: "Oh the last train didn't have a lot of seats so it must have been on the T2 railway line".

Which one of the following sentences shows the mistake Tara made?

A Not all old trains are on the T2 railway line

B The trains on the T2 line are different from other old trains

C There may be more than one train on the T2 line

D The trains may be different on that day

16 Three golf balls are lined up in the middle of the field, they are either yellow or grey.

Adam hits the yellow ball and it rolls to the ball in the middle which moves the last ball which is grey.

On the basis of this information, which one of the following statements must be true?

A There is only one yellow ball

B There is only one grey ball

C A yellow ball hit a grey ball

D A grey ball hit a yellow ball

17 Victoria is at the fridge. She has to choose the ice cream tub without the spoon in it.

Peter gives her 5 clues to help her choose a tub.

- The strawberry ice cream is not next to the mint or lemon ice cream.
- The vanilla ice cream is to the left of the lemon one
- The chocolate ice cream is not next to the jar without the spoon
- The mint ice cream is at the far right and 2 places away from the lemon ice cream
- The lemon ice cream is 2 places away from the ice cream without the spoon

Which juice should Victoria choose?

A Strawberry

B Chocolate

C Mint

D Lemon

18 In a horse race, Blue Ribbon finishes 15 m ahead of Black Diamond who was 10 m behind Pink Bonbon.

White Cloud won the race 7 m ahead of Gold Champagne, who was 3 m behind Blue Ribbon.

Who came third in the race?

A Gold Champagne

B Black Diamond

C Pink Bonbon

D Blue Ribbon

19 A teacher says: "Every child should learn the phone numbers of their parents".

Which one of the following statements, if true, best supports the teacher's rule?

A This means the parents can call the child if they ever get lost
B This means if a child is ever hurt or in danger, the adult can call their parents
C Phone numbers are very long and hard to remember for small children
D Children may mix up the phone numbers of their parents

20 When Anna was trying out for the volleyball team, the coach told her "To have a chance at making the team, you must train with the Division 1 team at least twice every week".

If Anna's coach is right, which one of the following statements will be true?

A Everyone that turns up to the trainings will make the team
B None of the students that didn't turn up to trainings will make the team
C Some of the students that only turned up sometimes will make the team
D Only students that were in the team last year will make the team this year

21 Dennis and Jonathan arranged a time to meet to play tennis.

Dennis arrived 25 minutes late.

Jonathan arrived 15 minutes early.

Dennis arrived at 12:30 pm.

At what time did Jonathan arrive?

A 1:10 pm
B 12:00 pm
C 12:50 pm
D 11:50 am

22

> Rashay lost his phone on the school oval at lunch time. He told his friend Kourtney to look for a phone with a light blue case connected to a pair of black earphones.

Kourtney: "This has to be Rashay's phone, I found it on the school oval and it has the light blue case he was telling me about!"

Landen: "You won't know if his phone is for sure until you ask him!"

If the information in the box is true, whose reasoning is correct?

A Kourtney only

B Landen only

C Both Kourtney and Landen

D Neither Kourtney nor Landen

23 Mr Ping: "I know that 14 of my students have blue pencil cases, but I only saw 6 students with blue pencil cases in class today. That must mean the rest of the class has bought new pencil cases".

Which one of the following sentences shows the mistake Mr Ping has made?

A He did not count the students correctly

B He may not be in the right classroom

C Some students might have forgotten their pencil cases today

D Mr Ping may have taken over a different class today

24 The average height of students in a class is 120 cm. Jonathan, Dennis, Andrew and Darren are students in this class.

Their heights are given in the table.

Student	Height (cm)
Jonathan	135
Dennis	125
Andrew	105
Darren	115

One of these students is leaving school.

As a result, the average height of this class will become 125 cm.

Who is leaving school?

A Jonathan

B Dennis

C Andrew

D Darren

25 Clinton, Kane, Kanye and Kylie are sitting in a row on the train seats.

In, two of them are facing forwards and two are facing backwards.

Two have aisle seats and the other two have window seats.

I know that:
- Kane is next to Clinton
- Clinton is sitting diagonally opposite Kanye
- Kylie is facing forwards

Which one of the following do I also know?

A Clinton is sitting opposite Kylie

B Kanye is sitting facing backwards

C Kanye has a window seat

D Kane has an aisle seat

26 Peach believes that: "The local post office should stock a bigger range of stamps".

Which one of these statements, if true, best supports Peach's argument?

A More stamps to choose from will make buyers happier and more interested
B It is very expensive for the post office to invest in more stamps
C Many people never use stamps from the post office
D Some people do not care what stamp they use on their letters

27 Simon had 64 small white cubes.

He glued them together to make this solid. He then painted all faces of the solid blue.

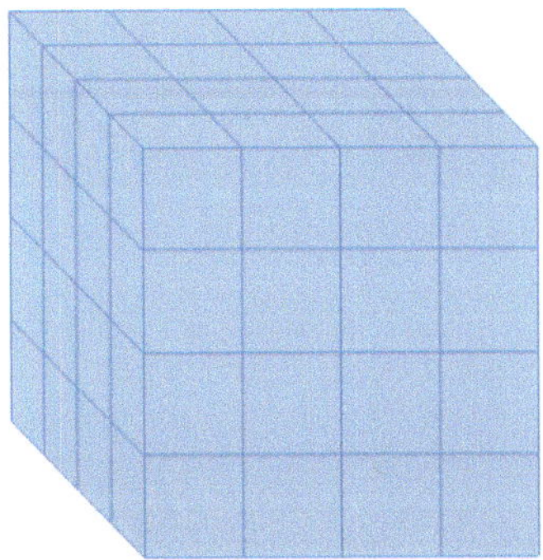

How many small cubes were **not** painted blue?

A 2
B 4
C 6
D 8

28

> When the intruder alert goes off, there could be someone breaking into Jackie's house or it could be a false alarm set off by her brother forgetting the password.

Jackie: "If you hear the intruder alert go off it might just be my brother".

Mikey: "Yes, but we never know it might be an intruder".

If the information in the box is true, whose reasoning is true?

A Jackie only
B Mikey only
C Both Jackie and Mikey
D Neither Jackie nor Mikey

29 Which one of the following four shapes will fit together with the shape below to form an isosceles triangle?

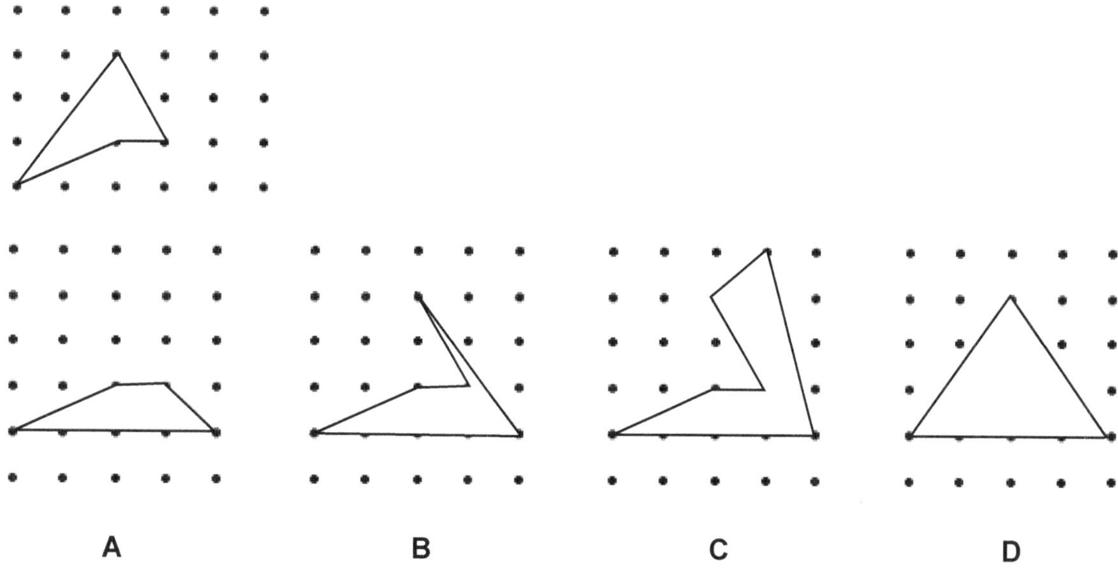

30 100 people were asked to pick a favourite sport out of soccer, cricket, golf and netball.

The survey results were as follows:

Soccer	40
Cricket	30
Golf	10
Netball	20

Which pie chart represents this information?

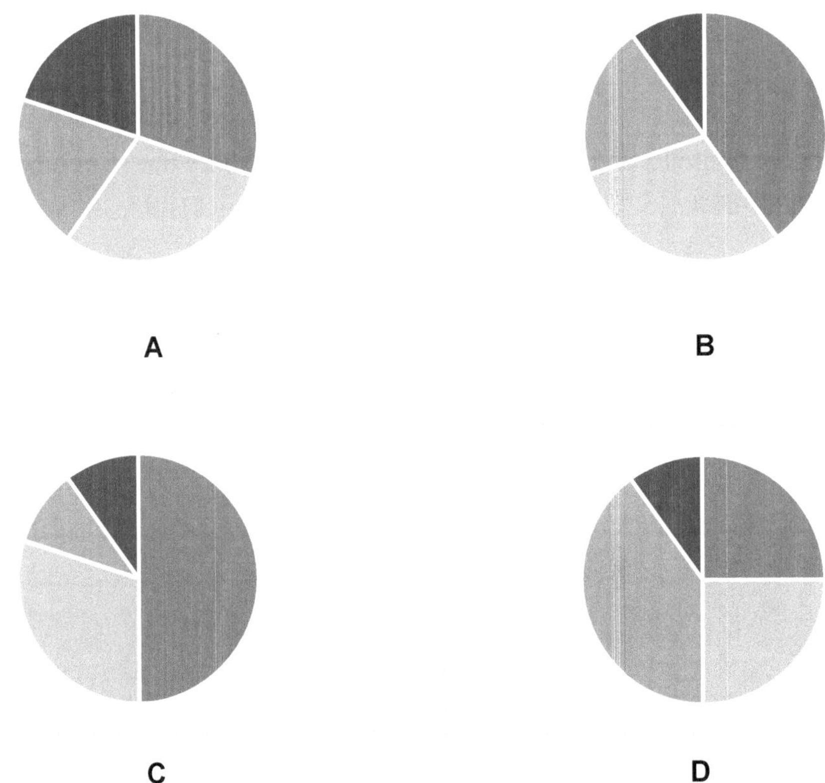

OC Practice Test Paper

Thinking Skills 10 (Time allowed: 30 min)

INSTRUCTIONS

1. Write your Name on the cover page.
2. There are **30** questions in this paper. For each question there are four possible answers, **A**, **B**, **C** and **D**. Choose the **one** correct answer and record your choice on the separate answer sheet. If you make a mistake, erase thoroughly and try again.
3. You will **not** lose marks for incorrect answers, so you should attempt **all 30** questions
4. You **must** complete the answer sheet within the time limit. There will **not** be any extra time at the end of the exam to record your answers on the answer sheet.
5. You can use the question paper for working out, but no extra paper is allowed.
6. Calculators and dictionaries are **NOT** allowed.

Name: ______________________________

1 Ann, Sasi, Lin and Mia went to a fair.

Ann had $5 and spent $3.50.

Sasi had $10 and spend $7.50.

Lin had $15 and spent $10.

Mia had $20 and spent $10.

Which girl spent the largest fraction of the money she had?

A Ann
B Sasi
C Lin
D Mia

2 Millie thinks that every student should get to choose what they want to do in their spare time in class instead of everyone doing art.

Which one of these statements, if true, best supports Millie's idea?

A This will mean students do not work together on projects
B There are too many students to let everyone choose something different
C This means not everyone has to do art if they don't like to
D It will make it hard for teachers to mark student progress

3 Nick, Ozan and Prince all have different, patterned fabrics in their boxes.

Nick has flowers, spotty, striped, and checkered.

Ozan has plain, checkered and striped.

Prince has butterflies, striped, cherries, and checkered.

Which pattern does Nick have that neither Ozan nor Prince has?

A Butterflies and cherries
B Flowers and spotty
C Plain and flowers
D Checkered and spotty

4 Every student gets to choose one fruit-flavoured smelly pen.

I get to choose one from each of the lists:

List 1:	**List 2:**	**List 3:**	**List 4:**
Kiwi	Banana	Banana	Lemon
Strawberry	Lemon	Strawberry	Grapefruit
Pear	Grape	Grapefruit	Orange
Orange	Cherry	Peach	Peach

I know I want banana, pear and grapefruit smelly pens.

Which of the following can I **not** choose as the flavour of my last smelly pen?

A Peach

B Grapefruit

C Orange

D Kiwi

5

Only people that are on their full driver's license can drive over 100 km/hr.

Robert: "Mary drove at 110 km/hr today so she must be on her full driver's license".

Johno: "She might have been speeding illegally and not be on her full driver's license".

If the information in the box above is true, whose reasoning is correct?

A Robert only

B Johno only

C Both Robert and Johno

D Neither Robert nor Johno

6 Jesslyn, Kris and Liam are lined up in a straight line.

If Jesslyn is to the right of Kris and Liam is to the left of Jesslyn, which one of the following statements much be true?

A Kris is furthest to the right

B Jesslyn is in the middle

C Liam is the furthest to the left

D Jesslyn is furthest to the right

7 Darrel, Wayne, Ari and Lucia each play different sports.

Wayne and Ari both dislike basketball and soccer, and Lucia is not tall enough to do basketball.

Wayne dislikes volleyball while Ari dislikes badminton.

Which of the following is true?

A Darrel plays volleyball and Lucia plays soccer

B Lucia plays soccer and Wayne plays badminton

C Ari plays badminton and Wayne plays volleyball

D Ari plays volleyball while Lucia plays basketball

8

Ayush and Akesh are on the soccer field.

Akesh: "The only people allowed on the soccer field right now are Year 12 students and teachers. This means that hat on the floor must belong to someone in year 12 or a teacher".

Which one of the following sentences shows the mistake Akesh made?

A The hat may have been there for a long time and belong to another grade

B Ayush and Akesh might have gotten the times wrong

C There may be more than one grade on the field at this time

D The other students in this grade might not wear hats

9 A lollipop man says: "Every parent should make sure that their child uses the zebra crossing to cross the road".

Which one of the following statements, if true, best supports the lollipop man's idea?

A This means parents know where their children are and if they are coming to school

B This means the man can make sure students are wearing a uniform

C Most children run across streets without checking for cars properly

D Children may not listen to the lollipop man so their parents must tell them

10 Jason opened up a piece of paper he made holes in and it looked like this.

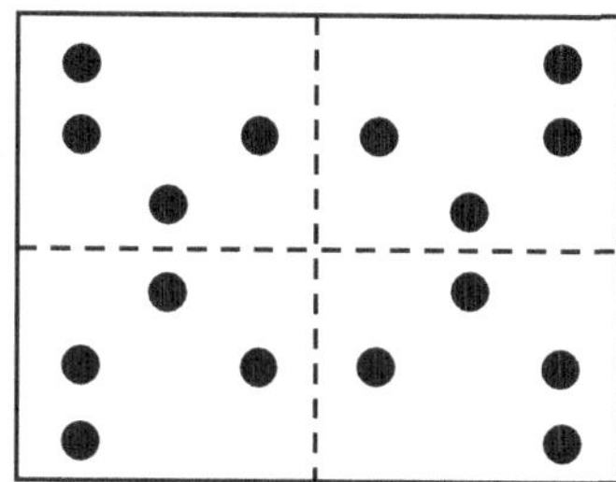

Choose how he had punched holes in the paper when folded.

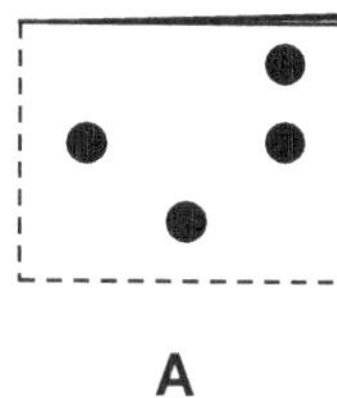

A

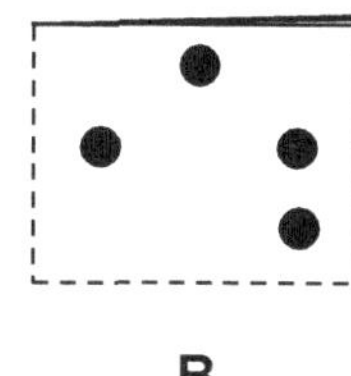

B

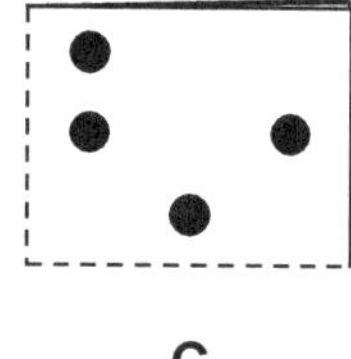

C

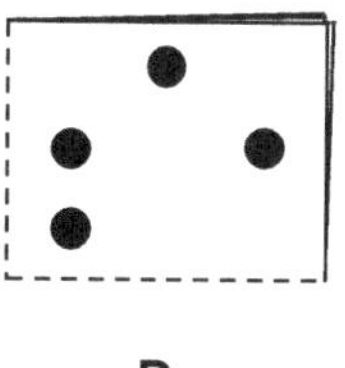

D

11 Kimmy's teacher told her that she has great potential to be one of the greatest scientists of all time but to do that she must pass the end of year science exam. She said, "To even have a chance at passing the exam you must revise your work and do practice exams at least twice a week".

If Kimmy's teacher is right, which one of the following statements will be true?

A Everyone that does practice tests twice a week will pass the exam

B None of the people that don't do practice exams will pass the test

C Some of the people that only do practices sometimes will pass

D Only people that practice once a week can pass the exam

12

> Chapman and Jessie were walking when they saw a big, white dog run past them into the dog park across the street. A man approaches them five minutes later.

The man: "Hi have you guys seen my dog, he's big, white and answers to Snowy."

Chapman: "Yes! We saw a big, white dog run past it might be yours".

Jessie: "We don't know if it's your dog for sure but it is very likely".

If the information in the box is true, whose reasoning is correct?

A Chapman only
B Jessie only
C Both Chapman and Jessie
D Neither Chapman nor Jessie

13 Choose the shape that joins with P to form a square.

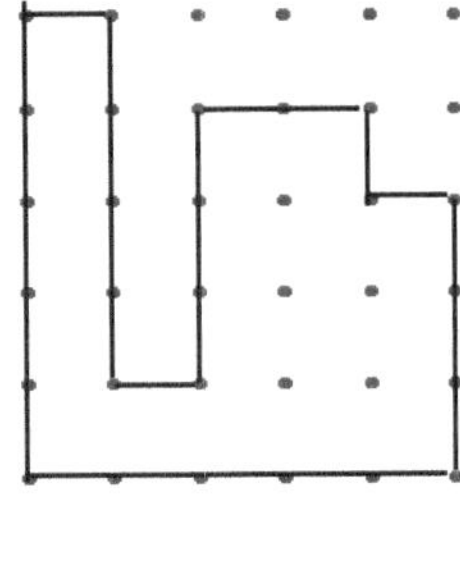

P

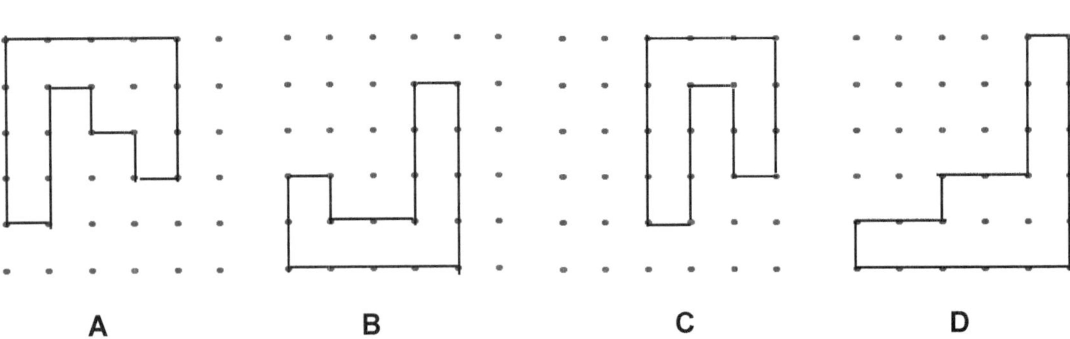

14 Vernon's music school has a competition each year to have their composition published by a major record label, being open to years 9 to 12.

Vernon: "I'll be able to compete in the composition this year since I will graduate in 5 years."

Which of the following sentences reveals Vernon's mistake?

A Compositions do not need to be original as long as it is remixed.

B Since the competition allows collaborations, students below year 9 will be able to compete.

C Only students who will graduate in three years will be able to compete.

D Vernon's music school will make exceptions for talented students below year 9.

15 Terry, Ashley, Ned and Sally are seated around a table on a train.

Two of them are facing forwards and two are facing backwards.

Two have aisle seats and the other two have window seats.

I know that:
- Ashley is next to Terry
- Terry is sitting diagonally opposite Ned
- Sally is facing forwards

Which one of the following do I also know?

A Ned is sitting opposite Sally

B Ned is sitting facing backwards

C Ned has a window seat

D Terry is sitting opposite Sally

16 Which graph shows the car which drove the longest distance without rest?

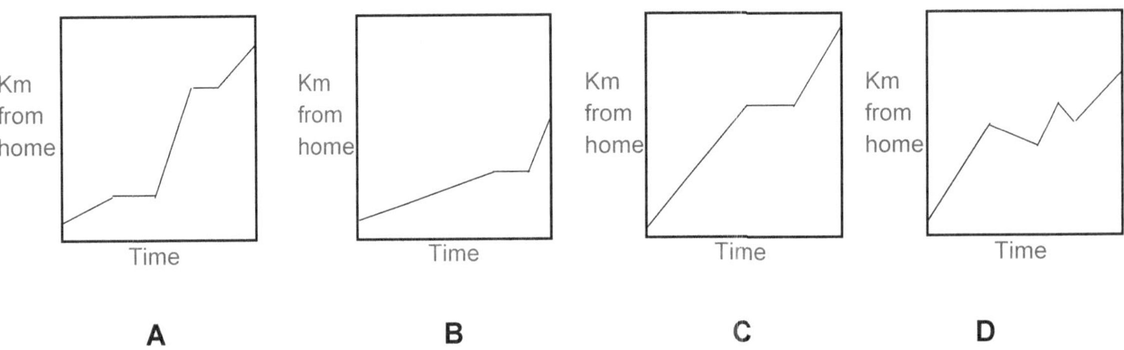

17 Hillary believes that: "We should start fining people more for littering".

Which one of these statements, if true, best supports Hillary's argument?

A This would mean less people would litter and damage the environment

B Some people will not be able to pay the increased littering fines

C Increased fines may mean increased backlash

D Some people do not want to pay more for these crimes

18

> When Felix the cat runs into the living room, it could be because it has started raining on the front porch.

Pam: "Felix just ran into the living room it must be raining outside".

Jim: "We don't know for sure, there may be a dog or some other reason for Felix running inside".

If the information in the box is true, whose reasoning is true?

A Pam only

B Jim only

C Both Pam and Jim

D Neither Pam nor Jim

19 The diagram shows three views of the same cube. One of the faces is blank.

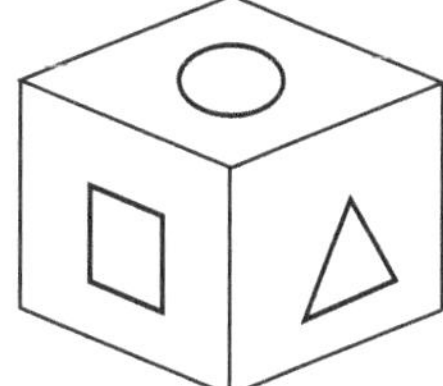
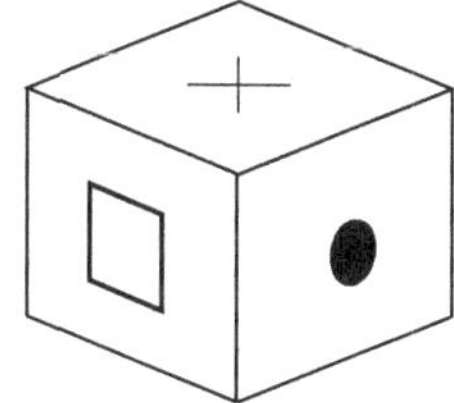
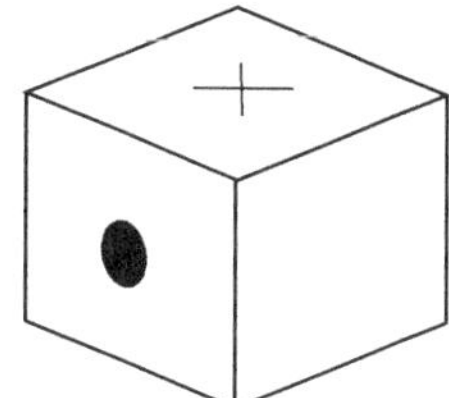

Which face is opposite the blank face?

A ●

B ╳

C ○

D □

20 Elis, Emma, Ed and Esra are in English class. Mrs Jamison announced that: "If Elis does not present tomorrow, then Emma will present. If Elis does present, then Ed will take Esra's place".

So, if Emma does not present tomorrow, which of the other three students will be presenting?

A Emma and Esra

B Ed and Esra

C Elis and Ed

D Elis only

21 Sara lives in a large city on the East Coast. Her younger cousin Marlee lives in the Midwest in a small town with fewer than 1,000 residents. Marlee has visited Sara several times during the past five years. In the same period of time, Sara has visited Marlee only once.

Based on the above information, which one of the following must be true?

A Sara is older than Marlee.

B Sara thinks small towns are boring.

C Marlee likes Sara better than Sara likes Marlee.

D Marlee wants to move to the East Coast.

22 One letter can only represent one number.

$$
\begin{array}{r}
ABC \\
\times \quad C \\
\hline
16BC
\end{array}
$$

What could be the value of C?

A 1 or 0
B 5 or 6
C 5 only
D 6 only

23 James lives north of Jess and north-west of Jane.

Jane lives north of Bill and west of William.

Jess lives east of Riley and north of Maya.

Who lives north-east of Maya?

A Jane
B James
C Maya
D Bill

24 Victoria believes that plastic bags should be banned completely from all supermarkets.

Which one of the following statements, if true, best supports Victoria's idea?

A Making bags from different materials would be very expensive
B This would mean less supermarkets will be able to give bags
C It would encourage more people to reuse bags and reduce pollution
D This would mean carrying groceries would be more difficult for shoppers

25 Which square is half shaded?

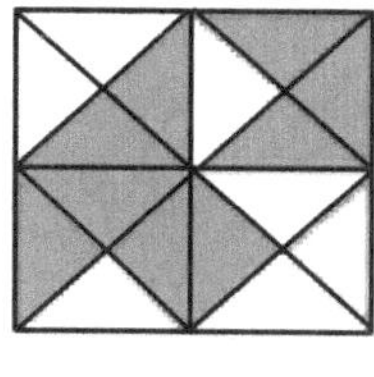
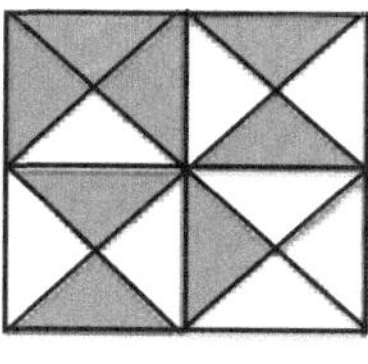

A **B** **C** **D**

26

> Whenever Bianca does not practice piano, her teacher makes her do extra lessons. When Bianca has to do extra lessons, she doesn't get to hang out at the park with her friends on Monday.

Katie: "Bianca didn't come to the park on Monday, she must not have practised on the piano enough".

Alexa: "Maybe she was just sick today, we don't know the reason for sure".

If the information in the box is true, whose reasoning is correct?

A Katie only
B Alexa only
C Both Katie and Alexa
D Neither Katie nor Alexa

27 Here are two identical equilateral triangles.

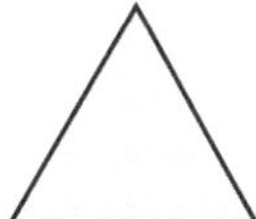
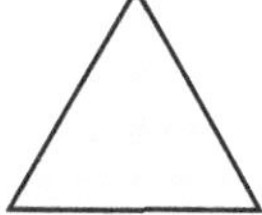

Which one of the following shapes can be made when these two triangles are joined together, side by side, without overlapping?

A trapezium
B rhombus
C triangle
D square

28 Three golf balls are lined up in the middle of the field, they are either blue or brown.

Nick hits the blue ball and it rolls to the ball in the middle which knocks the last brown ball.

On the basis of this information, which one of the following statements must be true?

A There is only one blue ball

B There is only one brown ball

C A blue ball hit a brown ball

D A brown ball hit a blue ball

29 Janice is at the farmer's market. She has to choose the cheapest fruit on sale.

Ben gives her 5 clues to help her choose a fruit to buy.

- The grapes are not next to the kiwis or mangoes
- The cherries are to the left of the mangoes
- The lychees are not next to the cheapest fruit
- The kiwis are on the far right and 2 places away from the mangoes
- The mangoes are 2 places away from the cheapest fruit

Which fruit should Janice buy?

A Grapes

B Cherries

C Mangoes

D Lychees

30 Polly's family is choosing a colour to paint their new wall.

They could vote to have yellow, purple or pink.

Everyone could only choose for one colour and the colour would only be chosen if everyone chose the same.

Knowing **one** of the following would allow us to know the result of the vote. Which one is it?

A Polly voted for purple

B No one voted for purple or pink

C Everyone voted for pink or purple

D Pink was the most popular vote

OC Practice Test Paper
Thinking Skills 6 – Answer Sheet

Fill in the appropriate circle for your chosen answer

Eg.. A B C D
○ ● ○ ○

Use a pencil. If you make a mistake, erase thoroughly and try again.

NAME : **SCORE:**

1	A B C D ○ ○ ○ ○	11	A B C D ○ ○ ○ ○	21	A B C D ○ ○ ○ ○
2	A B C D ○ ○ ○ ○	12	A B C D ○ ○ ○ ○	22	A B C D ○ ○ ○ ○
3	A B C D ○ ○ ○ ○	13	A B C D ○ ○ ○ ○	23	A B C D ○ ○ ○ ○
4	A B C D ○ ○ ○ ○	14	A B C D ○ ○ ○ ○	24	A B C D ○ ○ ○ ○
5	A B C D ○ ○ ○ ○	15	A B C D ○ ○ ○ ○	25	A B C D ○ ○ ○ ○
6	A B C D ○ ○ ○ ○	16	A B C D ○ ○ ○ ○	26	A B C D ○ ○ ○ ○
7	A B C D ○ ○ ○ ○	17	A B C D ○ ○ ○ ○	27	A B C D ○ ○ ○ ○
8	A B C D ○ ○ ○ ○	18	A B C D ○ ○ ○ ○	28	A B C D ○ ○ ○ ○
9	A B C D ○ ○ ○ ○	19	A B C D ○ ○ ○ ○	29	A B C D ○ ○ ○ ○
10	A B C D ○ ○ ○ ○	20	A B C D ○ ○ ○ ○	30	A B C D ○ ○ ○ ○

BLANK PAGE

OC Practice Test Paper
Thinking Skills 7 – Answer Sheet

Fill in the appropriate circle for your chosen answer

Eg.. A B C D
○ ● ○ ○

Use a pencil. If you make a mistake, erase thoroughly and try again.

NAME : **SCORE:**

1	A B C D ○ ○ ○ ○	11	A B C D ○ ○ ○ ○	21	A B C D ○ ○ ○ ○
2	A B C D ○ ○ ○ ○	12	A B C D ○ ○ ○ ○	22	A B C D ○ ○ ○ ○
3	A B C D ○ ○ ○ ○	13	A B C D ○ ○ ○ ○	23	A B C D ○ ○ ○ ○
4	A B C D ○ ○ ○ ○	14	A B C D ○ ○ ○ ○	24	A B C D ○ ○ ○ ○
5	A B C D ○ ○ ○ ○	15	A B C D ○ ○ ○ ○	25	A B C D ○ ○ ○ ○
6	A B C D ○ ○ ○ ○	16	A B C D ○ ○ ○ ○	26	A B C D ○ ○ ○ ○
7	A B C D ○ ○ ○ ○	17	A B C D ○ ○ ○ ○	27	A B C D ○ ○ ○ ○
8	A B C D ○ ○ ○ ○	18	A B C D ○ ○ ○ ○	28	A B C D ○ ○ ○ ○
9	A B C D ○ ○ ○ ○	19	A B C D ○ ○ ○ ○	29	A B C D ○ ○ ○ ○
10	A B C D ○ ○ ○ ○	20	A B C D ○ ○ ○ ○	30	A B C D ○ ○ ○ ○

BLANK PAGE

OC Practice Test Paper
Thinking Skills 8 – Answer Sheet

Fill in the appropriate circle for your chosen answer

Eg.. A B C D
○ ● ○ ○

Use a pencil. If you make a mistake, erase thoroughly and try again.

NAME : **SCORE:**

1	A B C D ○ ○ ○ ○	11	A B C D ○ ○ ○ ○	21	A B C D ○ ○ ○ ○
2	A B C D ○ ○ ○ ○	12	A B C D ○ ○ ○ ○	22	A B C D ○ ○ ○ ○
3	A B C D ○ ○ ○ ○	13	A B C D ○ ○ ○ ○	23	A B C D ○ ○ ○ ○
4	A B C D ○ ○ ○ ○	14	A B C D ○ ○ ○ ○	24	A B C D ○ ○ ○ ○
5	A B C D ○ ○ ○ ○	15	A B C D ○ ○ ○ ○	25	A B C D ○ ○ ○ ○
6	A B C D ○ ○ ○ ○	16	A B C D ○ ○ ○ ○	26	A B C D ○ ○ ○ ○
7	A B C D ○ ○ ○ ○	17	A B C D ○ ○ ○ ○	27	A B C D ○ ○ ○ ○
8	A B C D ○ ○ ○ ○	18	A B C D ○ ○ ○ ○	28	A B C D ○ ○ ○ ○
9	A B C D ○ ○ ○ ○	19	A B C D ○ ○ ○ ○	29	A B C D ○ ○ ○ ○
10	A B C D ○ ○ ○ ○	20	A B C D ○ ○ ○ ○	30	A B C D ○ ○ ○ ○

BLANK PAGE

OC Practice Test Paper
Thinking Skills 9 – Answer Sheet

Fill in the appropriate circle for your chosen answer

Eg.. A B C D
○ ● ○ ○

Use a pencil. If you make a mistake, erase thoroughly and try again.

NAME :

SCORE:

1	A B C D ○ ○ ○ ○	11	A B C D ○ ○ ○ ○	21	A B C D ○ ○ ○ ○
2	A B C D ○ ○ ○ ○	12	A B C D ○ ○ ○ ○	22	A B C D ○ ○ ○ ○
3	A B C D ○ ○ ○ ○	13	A B C D ○ ○ ○ ○	23	A B C D ○ ○ ○ ○
4	A B C D ○ ○ ○ ○	14	A B C D ○ ○ ○ ○	24	A B C D ○ ○ ○ ○
5	A B C D ○ ○ ○ ○	15	A B C D ○ ○ ○ ○	25	A B C D ○ ○ ○ ○
6	A B C D ○ ○ ○ ○	16	A B C D ○ ○ ○ ○	26	A B C D ○ ○ ○ ○
7	A B C D ○ ○ ○ ○	17	A B C D ○ ○ ○ ○	27	A B C D ○ ○ ○ ○
8	A B C D ○ ○ ○ ○	18	A B C D ○ ○ ○ ○	28	A B C D ○ ○ ○ ○
9	A B C D ○ ○ ○ ○	19	A B C D ○ ○ ○ ○	29	A B C D ○ ○ ○ ○
10	A B C D ○ ○ ○ ○	20	A B C D ○ ○ ○ ○	30	A B C D ○ ○ ○ ○

BLANK PAGE

OC Practice Test Paper
Thinking Skills 10 – Answer Sheet

Fill in the appropriate circle for your chosen answer

Eg.. A B C D
○ ● ○ ○

Use a pencil. If you make a mistake, erase thoroughly and try again.

NAME : **SCORE:**

1	A B C D ○ ○ ○ ○	11	A B C D ○ ○ ○ ○	21	A B C D ○ ○ ○ ○
2	A B C D ○ ○ ○ ○	12	A B C D ○ ○ ○ ○	22	A B C D ○ ○ ○ ○
3	A B C D ○ ○ ○ ○	13	A B C D ○ ○ ○ ○	23	A B C D ○ ○ ○ ○
4	A B C D ○ ○ ○ ○	14	A B C D ○ ○ ○ ○	24	A B C D ○ ○ ○ ○
5	A B C D ○ ○ ○ ○	15	A B C D ○ ○ ○ ○	25	A B C D ○ ○ ○ ○
6	A B C D ○ ○ ○ ○	16	A B C D ○ ○ ○ ○	26	A B C D ○ ○ ○ ○
7	A B C D ○ ○ ○ ○	17	A B C D ○ ○ ○ ○	27	A B C D ○ ○ ○ ○
8	A B C D ○ ○ ○ ○	18	A B C D ○ ○ ○ ○	28	A B C D ○ ○ ○ ○
9	A B C D ○ ○ ○ ○	19	A B C D ○ ○ ○ ○	29	A B C D ○ ○ ○ ○
10	A B C D ○ ○ ○ ○	20	A B C D ○ ○ ○ ○	30	A B C D ○ ○ ○ ○

BLANK PAGE

OC Practice Test Answers
Thinking Skills 6

Question	Answer	Explanation
1	D	The present can only be used while it is cold, takes some skill, and may injure the user. A Snowboard is the only present to fit this description.
2	B	Given that Norris likes lemons and Shirley likes oranges, Megan must like bananas.
3	C	Building a house is something that takes time and effort. The first pig put very little effort into making his house, leading to the assumption that he built his house poorly and therefore chose a bad material.
4	A	Each hour on a clock is separated by 30°. Angle A: 60° Angle B: 82.5° Angle C: 75° Angle D: 67.5°
5	D	Making a working laptop requires being good at both coding and hardware. Sally is not good with hardware so will not make a working laptop, as such Sam is wrong. Same is not good at coding so will not make a working laptop, meaning Sally is wrong.
6	B	Laroi is to the right of both Justin and Travis, meaning Option C is correct.
7	A	Jimmy says that Sally's laptop is grey, but does not say that her laptop is the only grey coloured one. Option A points out this mistake.
8	C	The number of piles is as follows: Dennis: $48 \div 4 = 12$ Jonathan: $72 \div 6 = 12$ Andrew: $65 \div 5 = 13$ Neil: $77 \div 7 = 11$

9	A	Drawing a diagram will help solve this question. Cale Barley Deli France Guernsey Elmo As such, Barley is northwest of Elmo
10	A	Person 1 views the shape from the top and Person 2 views it from the right. Both 1 and 2 have the correct view.
11	D	IF likes Burritos THEN likes Burgers IF likes Burgers THEN likes Pizza IF likes Burgers THEN doesn't like Tacos If Jess likes Burritos, then she also likes Burgers. Therefore she doesn't like Tacos and Option D is correct.
12	B	Sports specialists advocate for the use of helmets. Option B provides a reason for this statement so is correct. Although Option C is partially correct it is not the best answer, as balls pose a greater risk to batsmen than bats do.
13	C	Jenny believes that students should eat healthier meals instead of junk food. Option C is correct, as it strengthens the argument by providing a reason why healthier meals are better for students.
14	C	Ronaldo's coach states that knowing how to kick a goal is a requirement for the Portuguese team. As such, all players on the Portugal team must know how to kick a goal.
15	B	To make up over half the population, a group must take up more than half of the pie chart. 20-59 and 40 and over are the only two groups that make up over half the population.
16	B	

17	B	If the air conditioning is working, the temperature will be decreasing; and if it is broken, the temperature will be increasing. As such, the graph showing the correct temperature must initially be sloping down, and have two sections that slope up.
18	C	Vince: Toyota, Subaru, McLaren Brian: *Ferrari*, *Lamborghini*, Toyota Dom: *Lamborghini*, *Nissan*, Toyota
19	C	Harry's statement implies that he knows the release date of every Terry movie. Option A is irrelevant to his statement. Every movie has a name that doesn't change after release, so Options B and D are incorrect. Option C is then correct, as if there were two movies with the same name Harry would know which release date was right.
20	D	For the same number to be on opposite faces, the numbers must be exactly apart in a certain direction. Only Option D meets this criteria.
21	A	Both those in the top 5 and those that can prove that their bat was faulty will make it into the next round. However, there is no limit to the number of competitors that can prove that their bat was faulty. Option A points this mistake out.
22	A	Audi only appears in List 4, and Supra only appears in Lists 1 and 4; so the individual will pick a Supra from List 1 and an Audi from List 4. As Nissan only appears in List 1, it then cannot be selected.
23	A	Letty is diagonally opposite Jason, so Mia being next to Letty means that she is directly opposite Jason. As such, Snoop must be seated next to Jason and opposite Letty. Option A is correct.
24	C	The truth of statements can be worked out by checking the graph. The minimum average temperature was roughly 17°, meaning Option C is correct.

25	A	Leonard's argument implies that drawing will not be detrimental to becoming a physicist. Options C and D are incorrect as they do not cover the relationship between the drawing and physics. Option B is partially correct but not the best answer, as being famous would not assist in becoming a physicist. Option A best strengthens the argument, as practicing a skill that physicists use would assist him in becoming one.
26	B	One must be at least 130cm tall and not get sick easily to go on the ride. Option B is correct, as Adam fits these requirements so can go on the ride.
27	D	Alan plays OR Brenda plays IF Alan plays THEN Kalie plays As Brenda is not playing, Alan will play and then Kalie will play as well.
28	B	PewDiePie mentions that he knows all of the keys, but Ninja stated that fast building requires the keys to be *memorized*. Option B points out this mistake. If this answer is not immediately clear, the other options can all be ruled out as they do not relate to either statement.
29	C	Ron's ball hit one of the three bars, although it is not specified which one. Option C is the only correct answer, as ruling out the crossbar would mean that the ball hit either the left or right bar.
30	B	Daniel is 16 metres ahead of Ryan, Larry is 13 metres ahead, and Larry is only 9. Thus, Larry is in second place

OC Practice Test Answers
Thinking Skills 7

Question	Answer	Explanation
1	A	A pentagonal pyramid has a pentagon for the base and five triangles forming the top vertex. Its base has five edges and five vertices, and the sides have five edges and one vertex.
2	D	Using the clues, the formation is: Kitchen Andy Simon Holly Emma Living room Andy is opposite Holly, so Option D is correct.
3	C	The scientist claims that climate change threatens the survival of humans and animals alike. Option C states that climate change may end the survival of all species, thus strengthens the argument. Options A, B, and D all weaken the argument by downplaying climate change.
4	B	A student may be called into the Deputy Principal's office for one of two reasons. Jeremy assumes that there is only one potential reason for being called into the office, so is wrong. Ria points this mistake out, so is correct.
5	B	The first and second views establish that the square and cross are opposite from each other. Option B is the only option with this property.
6	A	

7	B	A graduate may receive the first job that they apply for, so applying for lots of jobs is not a requirement. As such, Option B is correct. It is worth noting that Option C is irrelevant to the statement, as it comments on time and stress rather than success in finding jobs.
8	C	Using the 2nd, 4th, 5th, and 6th statements, the friends' numbers are: Adolf: 1 Joseph: 2 Daisy: 3 Poppy: 4 Jennifer: 5
9	B	Each feature in the main shape will be matched by an opposite feature in the correct option, so if the main shape slopes outwards the correct option will slope inwards. Option B is the only one that matches the main shape.
10	B	
11	D	Neil is the only student to meet the requirements for both races.
12	D	The question states that ice-blocks are always the result of the school having extra money, and will always cause free time. However, free time is not always caused by the school spending extra money on ice blocks, so Daniel is incorrect. Josh's statement is also incorrect, as the school buying ice-blocks for students isn't greedy.
13	A	Option A shows the view from the left side. It is the only option that has four blocks along the base, so the other options are incorrect.
14	D	In these questions, it is important to remember that the logic only works in one direction. All oboe players are musicians, but this doesn't mean that all musicians are oboe players. Options A, B, and C would all require the logic to work in the opposite direction, so are incorrect.

15	A	Using the statements, the seating arrangement is: Ashley Bella Emily Caitlyn Danielle Caitlyn and Danielle must be in the second row, leaving Emily in the front right.
16	D	Given there are five students on either side of him, there are 6 columns. $48 \div 6 = 8$, meaning there are 8 rows. He is in the 7th row, meaning there are 6 rows in front of him.
17	C	Dentists state that brushing teeth twice and flossing once daily is effective in maintaining dental health. Options A, B, and D are all incorrect, as they state that regular brushing may either be ineffective or harmful. Option C is correct, as it is the only one to suggest that regular brushing is beneficial.
18	B	A: $42 > 21 + 21$ (False) B: $57 > 21 + 30$ (True) C: $30 > 57$ (False) D: $42 + 21 = 30 + 57 + 31 + 21 + 44$ (False)
19	D	Jamie: ice-cream, muffins, pizza John: fish, pie, pizza, pasta, muffins Mia: cookies, fish, soup, pizza, muffins
20	A	Painting and piano can both only be found in List 1. As such, Lisa cannot choose painting.
21	D	50 out of 100 cars were silver. Option D is the only one to have one section that takes up half of its pie chart.
22	B	

23	B	If a student returns their note, they will be able to attend the carnival. However, it isn't stated that every student to return their note will be allowed to attend; meaning Jason is incorrect. Luke is correct, as if Tony is unable to return his note he won't be allowed to attend.
24	D	Amy is in front of both Rishi and Bethany, meaning she is at the front of the line.
25	B	
26	A	
27	B	
28	C	
29	A	Parrots are the only birds with bright red and green feathers, so a bird matching this description must be a parrot. As such, Sasha is correct. However, parrots can be any length up to 25cm, so Alex is incorrect.
30	C	It is not stated that sickness is the only reason for a student's absence. Therefore a student may be absent for reasons, such as a sports carnival; and Option C is correct.

OC Practice Test Answers
Thinking Skills 8

<table>
<tr><th>Question</th><th>Answer</th><th>Explanation</th></tr>
<tr><td>1</td><td>C</td><td>The music teacher argues that learning an instrument is as important as playing sports. Option C provides a benefit of playing music, thus strengthening the argument. All other options weaken the argument by contradicting this point.</td></tr>
<tr><td>2</td><td>D</td><td>The table can be completed as follows:
<table>
<tr><td>Gender</td><td>For</td><td>Against</td><td>Unsure</td></tr>
<tr><td>Male</td><td>65</td><td>4</td><td>35</td></tr>
<tr><td>Female</td><td>55</td><td>16</td><td>25</td></tr>
<tr><td>Total</td><td>120</td><td>20</td><td>60</td></tr>
</table>
As there are 120 For and 60 Unsure, there must be 20 Against</td></tr>
<tr><td>3</td><td>B</td><td>Eve: Puma, Fila, Adidas
Kyle: Champion, New Balance, Gucci
Josh: *Nike*, Puma, Fila</td></tr>
<tr><td>4</td><td>D</td><td>A student must return the note at the meeting to be able to go on the excursion. Neither Taylor nor Bryce can attend the meeting, so they will not be able to go. As such, both statements are incorrect.</td></tr>
<tr><td>5</td><td>B</td><td>The toy sale raised $45. Option B shows this amount.</td></tr>
<tr><td>6</td><td>D</td><td>The order of the line from left to right is Noah, Josh, Blake.</td></tr>
<tr><td>7</td><td>B</td><td>Katy’s bag is black with a green bag, but there may also be other bags that fit this description. Option B points this mistake out.</td></tr>
</table>

8	A	Transport NSW recommends mask wearing. Option A provides a benefit of wearing a mask, so best strengthens the argument. Option D is also a benefit of mask wearing, however hiding from the police is against the interest of the NSW government; so the claim would not be made for this reason.
9	A	Drawing a flipped version of the shape will help answer this question. When the shape has been flipped, the upper curve will dip at the left edge and extend at the right edge. Option A reflects this.
10	D	Joseph's instructor argues that students must complete 10 practice papers to be able to receive a distinction. Option D best strengthens this argument, as it states that no student who hasn't completed all 10 has received a distinction.
11	D	A cricket bat is grey with stickers in the middle, however other bats may also fit this description. As such, George is incorrect. The bat in question is also sold in 15 countries, which is more than the 10 countries that cricket bats are sold in. Therefore, Amy is also incorrect.
12	D	Using only clues 1 and 4, it can be established that the shape in question is a square.
13	B	Although students have sports today, some may have forgotten their shoes or may be sitting out. Therefore students may be present but not wearing sports shoes, so Option B is correct.
14	C	Using the clues, the formation is: Forwards Stella Josh Macy Dax Backwards Josh is opposite Dax, so Option C is correct.

15	B	The environmentalist says that carbon pollution affects both us and animals. Option B states why we are both affected, thus strengthening the argument.
16	B	By drawing lines to segment the different shapes, it can be worked out that there is no trapezoid present in the question.
17	B	Nate dances OR Faran dances Nate and Steve OR David As Faran is not dancing, Nate and Steve will dance.
18	C	Shop 1: $\$4 + \$4 \times 50\% + \$4 = \$10$ Shop 2: $\$4 + \$0 + \$4 = \$8$ Shop 3: $\$3 + \$3 + \$0 = \$6$ Shop 4: $\$3 + \$3 + \$3 = \$9$
19	B	To pass the driving test, Scot must practice for at least two hours at a time, however he only practices an hour. Option B points out that increased frequency alone does not guarantee success, so is correct.
20	D	The easiest way to solve this question is to draw a diagram. V Z W Y A X Town Z is northwest of Town X
21	A	The car was parked for 4 hours and 30 minutes, which means they must pay the \$3 for the initial hour, and \$2 for the four partial hours after that.
22	A	The nutritionist claims that water is beneficial for children. Option A is correct as it outlines one of the benefits of drinking water.
23	B	In the question, the cube is rotated away from the viewer from one image to the next. Drawing a net of the cube using this understanding allows us to determine that Option B is the only correct answer.

24	B	The logic in the question identifies that rain will always lead to free time, but it does not state that rain is the only reason for free time. As such, Sam is incorrect but Joel is correct.
25	A	The health specialist that PDHPE is an important part of school. Option A provides a benefit of PHDPE education, thus strengthening the argument.
26	B	Kabir: cats, snakes, lizards Kylie: frogs, insects, dogs Parth: dogs, *birds*, *rats*, snakes
27	C	If Jenna has x marbles, then June has $6x$ marbles and Tom has $2x$ marbles. Jessie must have some amount greater than $2x$, as they have more marbles than Tom. Option C is correct.
28	B	If Kevin feels lethargic, he will not perform well and he cannot win. Option B is correct. It is important to note that he may eat badly but not feel lethargic; and also that he may perform well but still not win.
29	D	Thinking outside the box and attention to detail are both required to be a good architect. Pat does not have good attention to detail, and it is not mentioned that Josh has good creativity; so it cannot be stated with certainty that either will be a good architect. Both statements are incorrect.
30	C	Knowledge and time are required to complete the homework. If Amy does not have both, she cannot complete her homework, so Option C is correct.

OC Practice Test Answers
Thinking Skills 9

Question	Answer	Explanation
1	B	If no one voted for green or purple, then everyone must have voted for black. This is the only case in which we can know the result of the vote. It is important to note that Kimmy's class may only have three students, so we cannot know whether black was chosen or not in Option A.
2	B	After the turn, both Dennis and Andrew will be facing East.
3	D	Kris believes that younger children should be able to have gym memberships. Option D provides a benefit of this idea, so is correct.
4	C	Idris: cookies, vanilla, strawberry Jack: honey, strawberry, rocky road, vanilla Harry: *chocolate*, *mint*, strawberry, vanilla
5	A	The correct option will look like the top right of the unfolded shape. This is seen in Option A.
6	B	Cadie performs OR Catherine performs Cadie and Charles perform OR Chris performs If Catherine doesn't perform, then Cadie and Charles will perform.
7	D	Jessie believes that free knee pads should be available. Option D supports the argument by providing a benefit of knee pads.
8	D	It is established that an unclean classroom will always lead to shouting, however it is not stated that the only reason for yelling is an unclean classroom. As such, both statements are incorrect.
9	D	There are 12 students with black hair, 16 blond, 20 brown, and 5 red. As such, there are 53 students in total.

10	A	Photography can only be found on List 1, so must be chosen from here. History can also only be found on this list, so it cannot be chosen.
11	C	There would be two overlapping faces in Option C.
12	B	To enjoy the buffet, an individual must have met the volunteering requirements or paid $4. Jessie could have eaten at the buffet due to either reason, so Ben is incorrect and Claire is correct.
13	D	Both Elle and Frank are to the left of Dylan, so he must be the furthest right.
14	B	To identify the correct option, match up the bottom edge of the top view with the shape.
15	A	Dan says that older trains have less seats and that the trains on T2 are usually older. However older trains may be found on other lines, which is pointed out by Option A.
16	C	With the colour of the middle ball unknown, the order is as follows: Yellow -> ?? -> Grey If the middle ball is grey, yellow hits grey when 1 hits 2; and if the middle ball is yellow, yellow hits grey when 2 hits 3.
17	A	Using the clues, the order of the ice creams is as follows: Strawberry, Vanilla, Lemon, Chocolate, Mint The ice cream without the spoon is two away from lemon and not next to chocolate, so it must be strawberry.
18	A	White Cloud won the race, with Gold Champagne 7m behind. Gold Champagne was 3m behind Blue Ribbon, therefore also 2m ahead of Pink Bonbon. As such, Gold Champagne must have placed third.
19	B	The teacher argues that students should learn their parents' phone numbers. Option B best supports the argument by providing a benefit of children knowing these numbers.

20	B	The coach states that turning up to training is required to make the team. Therefore those who did not turn up to training will not make the team, and Option B is correct.
21	D	Dennis arrived at 12:30pm, 40 minutes after Jonathan. As such, Jonathan must have arrived at 11:50am
22	B	Although the phone Kourtney found has a light blue case, there were no black headphones so it is not certainly Rashay's phone. As such, Kourtney is incorrect and Landen is correct.
23	C	A student may not have their blue pencil case for reasons other than getting a new one, such as forgetting it. As such, Option C is correct.
24	C	The total height of the students will go from 480cm to 375cm when the student leaves. Therefore, it must be Andrew leaving.
25	A	Using the clues, the formation is: Forwards Clinton Kane Kylie Kanye Backwards Clinton is opposite Kylie, so Option A is correct.
26	A	Peach argues for a larger range of postage stamps. Option A provides a reason for having a larger range, thus supporting her argument.
27	D	The number of cubes not painted blue is the number not on the edges, which is $2^3 = 8$
28	C	The alarm could be set off by an intruder or Jackie's brother. Jackie and Mikey each state one potential option, and they are both correct as they do not state that the other option is impossible.

29	B	An isosceles triangle must have only two sides of equal length. Although Options A, B, and C all form a triangle; Option B is the only one to form an isosceles triangle.
30	B	Soccer and Golf, and Cricket and Netball both add up to half the graph. Additionally, the two halves will have different size segments. Option B is the only one to fit these criteria.

OC Practice Test Answers
Thinking Skills 10

Question	Answer	Explanation
1	B	Ann spent 3/10 of the money Sasi spent 3/4 of the money Lin spend 2/3 of the money Mia spent 1/2 of the money Therefore, Sasi spent the largest fraction of the money
2	C	We want an answer that gives a reason that supports the statement. Option A is irrelevant to the statement. Options B and D opposes the statement. Option C is the answer, as it supports the idea that people should be able to do something other than art.
3	B	From comparing Nick with Ozan and Prince, we can see that flowers and spotty are patterns only Nick has.
4	D	Pear only appears in list 1, which means that the fruits on this list, if not repeated in other lists cannot be chosen. Kiwi, Option D, is present in this list but not in others. If you play out all the possibilities, you will also see that Options A, B and C cannot be the answer.
5	B	Robert is incorrect as there is a flaw in his argument. Mary might have illegally driven at 110km/hr without a full driver's licence. Following this reasoning, Johno's statement is correct.
6	D	The lineup is as follows: Kris Liam Jesslyn

<table>
<tr><td>7</td><td>B</td><td><table><tr><th></th><th>Darrel</th><th>Wayne</th><th>Ari</th><th>Lucia</th></tr><tr><td>Basketball</td><td>✓</td><td>×</td><td>×</td><td>×</td></tr><tr><td>Soccer</td><td></td><td>×</td><td>×</td><td></td></tr><tr><td>Volleyball</td><td></td><td>×</td><td></td><td></td></tr><tr><td>Badminton</td><td></td><td></td><td>×</td><td></td></tr></table>
If someone dislikes a sport, it is assumed that they do not play it. From the information given in the question, we can figure out, out of the process of elimination that Wayne plays badminton and Lucia plays soccer, and Ari plays volleyball.</td></tr>
<tr><td>8</td><td>A</td><td>Options B and C are statements inconsistent with the idea that the only people in the field right now are Year 12 students. Option D is illogical, as there is the possibility that Year 12 students also do not wear hats. Option A is the only logical answer.</td></tr>
<tr><td>9</td><td>C</td><td>We want an answer that confirms the importance of children using the zebra crossing. The obvious reason is that it, in some ways, promotes safety. Options A, B and D are not consistent with the purpose of zebra crossings. Only C is logical.</td></tr>
<tr><td>10</td><td>A</td><td>The dotted lines refer to parts where the paper is folded. Only Option A's pattern of dots corresponds with the top right corner.</td></tr>
<tr><td>11</td><td>B</td><td>Option A is incorrect as people who do the practice test twice a week AND revise their work have a chance at passing the exam. Passing isn't guaranteed. Similarly then, C and D are also incorrect. Option B is correct as it follows the logic of the question. If only those who revise their work and do practice exams twice a week, have a chance, but those who don't have any chance at all.</td></tr>
<tr><td>12</td><td>C</td><td>Chapman is correct, as he says the dog might be yours. He's correct, as the noted characteristics (big, white dog) do match.
Similarly then, Jessie is also correct. It might not be the man's dog but it is very likely it is.</td></tr>
<tr><td>13</td><td>B</td><td>Only Option B, when rotated 180 degrees clockwise can fit perfectly into Shape P.</td></tr>
</table>

14	C	Options A, B and D do not fit into the logic of the statement. Vernon's mistake was that he assumed that he would be able to compete as long as he hasn't graduated from high school. The answer closest to this is C.
15	D	The diagram should be as follows: Terry Ashley Sally Ned
16	D	The rest is shown in graphs as a straight horizontal line. Options A, B and C all show that the car has stopped throughout the trip. Option D shows that the car drove without rest. Therefore the answer is D.
17	A	We want a statement that supports fining people for littering. Options B, C and D oppose the idea of fining people. Only Option A fulfils the criteria.
18	B	The statement says that when Felix runs into the living room it could be because it was raining. This could mean there is a chance, but it is not definite. This makes Pam incorrect because his statement was that it must be raining outside. There could be other factors in play here. This makes Jim's statement correct. Therefore the answer is Jim only.
19	D	If you look at Cube 2 and Cube 3 you will notice that the X and black dots are repeating symbols on both cubes. Cube 2 is Cube 3 but rotated one time to the left. From this, you can tell that the white square is behind the blank face by checking both cubes.
20	C	If Elis is not present Emma will be. Vice versa also works. Therefore, Elis will be present. If Elis is present, Ed will also be but not Esra.
21	A	Insufficient information available for Options B, C and D. Option A is correct, as Marlee is said to be Sara's younger cousin, therefore Sara must be older.

22	C	C cannot represent zero, because it would make everything in the equation equal to zero, therefore Option A cannot be the answer. C cannot represent six, otherwise, 16BC will be written as 1CBC. After the process of elimination, only 5 can be the answer.
23	A	The diagram should be as follows: James Riley Jess Jane William Maya Bill
24	C	We want a reason for why plastic bags are bad, hence why they should be banned. Only C fulfils this requirement.
25	B	The number of triangles in one square is 16. The half-shaded square has 8 triangles coloured in.
26	B	Katie is incorrect as there can be other variables at play. Bianca not practising enough could be a reason, but it doesn't always have to be due to this. Following this logic, Alexa is correct.
27	B	The two triangles can be joined by rotating the second one slightly to fit against the first. When this happens, it will be a rhombus, as there will be 4 sides and all will be of equal length.
28	C	Insufficient information for Option A or B to be true. Option C is correct, as the question states that the middle ball knocked a brown ball. This means that the brown ball must have been the one hit.
29	A	Here, the fruit Janet should buy is the cheapest one. The order will be as follows: Grapes Cherries Mangoes Lychees Kiwis Either the Kiwi or Grape is the cheapest fruit (two places from the mango). Because Kiwi isn't an answer in options, A is the answer.

30	B	Everyone must vote for the same colour for that colour to be chosen. Only Option B allows us to know the result of the vote, as if no one voted for purple or pink, that means everyone voted for yellow.